PRAISE FOR *THE INTERACTIVE CLASS*

"Looking to transform your classroom? *The InterACTIVE Class* provides a blueprint that's based on psychology, technology, and actual classroom practice. The Merrills' Interactive Method—Prepare, Innovate, Visualize, Observe, Troubleshoot—will empower you with the framework you need. Your students are going to love the ideas you gather from this book! "

—Matt Miller, educator, speaker, author of *Ditch That Textbook*

"In their new book, the Merrills provide actionable ideas that place value on student choice and voice. I love how they take readers through their interACTIVE method of teaching with guiding questions and classroom examples. If you're interested in renewing your enthusiasm for teaching and learning, definitely check out this book!"

—Monica Burns, EdD, author of *Tasks Before Apps,*
and founder of ClassTechTips.com

"*The InterACTIVE Class* has done it, y'all! The Merrills illustrate how primary and elementary classrooms can combine powerful teaching with digital tools to create engaging classrooms where learning comes first. Each chapter offers actionable ideas that will inform, inspire, and bring about change in the classroom. *The InterACTIVE Class* will change your thinking and practice for the better!"

—Kasey Bell, author of *Shake Up Learning*

"This book is a friendly invitation for teachers to try new things to reach today's kids. The Merrills expertly marry teaching goals with avenues for accomplishing those goals. They articulate reasons and context for using today's popular digital tools. Their clever lessons are full of ways to combine standards with modern teaching practices—lessons you can use tomorrow!"

—Tony Vincent, educator, founder of Learning in Hand

"Since the moment that I first followed Joe and Kristin's work on Twitter, I not only wished that my own children were in their classes, but that I was in one of their classes myself! That same energy and passion for education shine through in *The InterACTIVE Class*. Whether you are a new teacher or an old dog looking to learn some new tricks, this book will first convince you to get more interactive and then lead you on a resource-filled, idea-rich journey to pull it off!"

—Jake Miller, @JakeMillerTech, #EduDuctTape Podcast and Twitter Chat host

"Within the pages of this book, Joe and Kristin Merrill share ideas, insights, and lesson examples that will transform your classroom to make learning come alive! *The InterACTIVE Class* offers creative ways to shift instruction, empower learners with engaging strategies, and help educators see new possibilities for amplifying student voice. This book is a must-read and will inspire you with practical advice to level up the fun for both teaching and learning."

—Ann Kozma, @annkozma723, educator innovation lead at Flipgrid

'Learning needs to be authentic and relevant to students. *The InterACTIVE Class* breathes life into education in a way which empowers teachers, students, and parents alike. This book is a MUST for anyone wondering, 'How can I better meet the needs of my learners?' giving specific lessons, ideas, models and, tools to immediately implement into any classroom."

—Julie Smith, @JGTechieTeacher, K–5 edtech consultant, blogger at *The Techie Teacher*®

THE
INTERACTIVE
CLASS

USING TECHNOLOGY TO MAKE LEARNING
MORE RELEVANT AND ENGAGING
IN THE ELEMENTARY CLASS

FOREWORD BY DR. CHARLIE MILLER

JOE AND KRISTIN MERRILL

Published by ElevateBooksEdu

Editing, Cover Design, and Interior Design by My Writers' Connection

Library of Congress Control Number: On File
Paperback ISBN: 978-1-7334814-5-8
Ebook ISBN: 978-1-7334814-6-5

First Printing: January 2020

DEDICATION

To our sons, Bryson and Baxson, thank you for grounding
us and keeping us distracted with your humor.

To all of the teachers in our family,
thank you for your love and support.

To our dear friend Greg, thank you for believing in us and
teaching us how to share the view inside our classroom.

And to all of our fellow colleagues, thank you for
inspiring, challenging, and supporting us.

CONTENTS

PART TWO: THE INTERACTIVE CLASS: ENGAGING APPS AND LESSONS

FOREWORD

Being an educator is a profession, a lifestyle, and a life's mission that is shaping the future of our beautiful planet more than any other. In the technology world, corporate statements are often fueled with extraneous synonyms and catchphrases for "changing the world," and some, indeed, are helping in this feat. Educators, on the other hand, should wake up every morning and know they are making a difference, know they are empowering the future leaders of tomorrow, and know they are profoundly changing the world one learner at a time.

Educators know that *being an educator* does not simply exist within the neat bounds of school bell to school bell. Being an educator is alarm clock to alarm clock. It infuses your dreams, energizes those precious few minutes to yourself between classes, and ignites ideas that you cannot wait to share with your colleagues across the hallway or halfway around the world. However, sometimes amongst the slides, the gradebooks, the meetings, and the numbers it's possible to lose sight of the extraordinary impacts of your work.

I can't think of anything more impactful than helping someone learn. Every single day hundreds of millions of learners are touched by the work and dedication of educators like you. Whether it is a fifth grader nervously preparing for their first presentation in front of the class, a kindergartener learning to write their name with freshly opened crayons, a seventh grader staying up late to put that last stroke of brilliance on their paper, or a freshman in high school realizing that "I can do this!" … Eyes light up, smiles widen, tears fall, doubts fade, and dreams expand. Educators fuel human curiosity and create opportunities that echo across decades in students' lives.

Great educators know that learning is an enduring and collaborative experience, not a checkbox at the completion of each lesson. That's likely why you are a few pages into this remarkable book focused on active, experiential learning. From freeing an educator stuck in a video game to rolling dice aligned with Flipgrid Topics to a QR code scavenger hunt throughout books in the library, the learning experiences shared across these pages all accomplish three essential pedagogical elements: They **engage** students. They **amplify** students' voices. And they **empower** students to believe they can accomplish the unimaginable.

Whether your use of technology in the classroom is excitingly recent or proudly well seasoned, it's always good to stop and reflect on your own pedagogical journey as an educator. Take yourself back to that first Tweet or Instagram post that inspired a new lesson, the first time you opened your laptop and envisioned a new project that would transform your students' thinking, or the first time you saw your students' eyes brighten with astonishment and pride as they realized the endless possibilities of their own creativity. These are the wonderful moments illustrated beautifully throughout the active learning experiences in this book.

As with all new endeavors, it's important to remember this simple yet powerful foundation. The interACTIVE class is not a destination. It's a journey. And on this journey, you are fortunate to have two inspiring, world-class guides in Kristin and Joe.

Before you turn the page and embark on this adventure, I'd like to say, **"THANK YOU!"** Thank you for everything you do every minute of every day of every year as an educator. It's not about the technology. It's not about the numbers. It's all about them: The students.

It's a privilege and an honor to welcome you to *The InterACTIVE Class*.

—Dr. Charlie Miller
founder, partner general manager of Flipgrid at Microsoft

PART ONE

INTRODUCTION

MEET YOUR INTERACTIVE GUIDES

INTRODUCTION *NOUN*

\ ˌin-trə-ˈdək-shən \

A FORMAL PRESENTATION OF ONE PERSON TO ANOTHER, IN WHICH EACH IS TOLD THE OTHER'S NAME

@TheMerrillsEDU

USE THE FLIPGRID APP TO OPEN UP A LIVE INTERACTIVE VIDEO SUMMARY OF EACH CHAPTER.

Congratulations and kudos to you for choosing to be a teacher—often described as the best profession in the world! The word *teacher* is defined as "one who teaches" and, while teachers *do* teach, this definition is rather ambiguous and anticlimactic when you consider how the profession of teaching has evolved over the last century and how the ideals and ideas surrounding education have shifted and changed. Whether you are new to the classroom this year or have been teaching for decades, you have probably played (or *will* play) many of these roles in addition to your role as *teacher*.

Nurse	Art Director	Mentor
Parent	Mediator	Health Instructor
IT Specialist	Web Designer	Scheduling Coordinator
Caregiver	Custodian	Nutritionist
Miracle Worker	Interpreter	Craft Coordinator
Counselor	Manager	Superhero
Editor	Discipline Officer	Office Manager
Comedian	Role Model	Multitasker
Therapist	Data Analyst	
Party Planner	Instructional Coach	

As you also likely know, teachers are often lifted onto pedestals by some while laid out on the chopping block by others. Some days you may feel you've been thrown to the sharks as your twenty-five students circle around you in the classroom. On other days you may feel you've just ridden a roller coaster upside down and backwards ten times in a row! Still other days you'll feel all you can do is tread water and stay afloat. Teaching is not always easy, and it is almost always messy and convoluted. But the rewards you reap in return make the crazy adventure worth it!

PATHS TO TEACHING

Teaching is beautiful because it is rooted in a desire to learn and a hope to lead others to do the same. And teaching doesn't look the same in any two places; no two classrooms, schools, or districts are exactly alike. Classrooms come in all shapes and sizes—just like the students inside them. They're all diverse and unique. The methods, materials, and mindsets teachers use and share appear similar—even uniform—when viewed as a big picture, but these also differ depending on the time and place.

The path people take to the profession differs as well. Some grow up knowing they aspire to teach and find themselves in their first classroom shortly after graduation. Others pursue an entirely different career—maybe in accounting or advertising—and over time decide they want more from life, leading them into a classroom, where they can use the specialized skill set from their prior career. Regardless of the path teachers take to the classroom, every one of them walks in with the same goal: to foster a love of learning while inspiring students to become lifelong learners.

KRISTIN

I am one of *those* teachers—the ones who grew up aspiring to teach. My grandmother was a primary school teacher in the 1940s, my mother was a high school Social Studies teacher, and both of my sisters taught elementary-aged children. I never doubted I wanted to grow up and have a job related to children. As a child, I "played school" with my dolls, giving each its own chair and assignment. As I grew up, I specifically took jobs placing me with different aged children, giving me various responsibilities to help dial in exactly what I wanted to do. Soon I was convinced I was called to teach. People said I was a "natural." By my senior year in high school, I had already banked a semester of college credits, and I was elated to be accepted into one of the state's best education programs. I worked hard, taking the maximum amount of credits every semester. Since I knew what I wanted to do, staying at college any longer than necessary seemed a silly waste of time—and money!

As a member of the college of education, I interned in various classrooms and mentored students every semester, giving me experience in every type of classroom I could imagine: primary, intermediate, co-teaching models, low income, private, etc. This varied experience continued as I graduated with my master's degree and headed off to accept my first position midway through the school year. As a schoolwide tutor for English language learners, I spent the first six months out of college getting my feet wet visiting various classrooms, seeing different teaching styles, and learning classroom management strategies. When the school year concluded, I settled in fourth grade and have taught this age of students ever since—in varying classroom models including standalone, co-teaching, ESE, and gifted.

But if I am being honest, despite all this experience and being so focused on what I wanted to do and where I wanted to teach, I still remember how I felt on my first day with my first "real" class. I was absolutely *terrified*. I struggled through my first year. I had difficulty planning content, managing my time, and learning how to navigate through developing relationships with my students. I also struggled because I had to take on all that my degrees *didn't* teach me about teaching. I never had a class that taught me how to pull off a room transformation. There was never a lesson that covered what to do when a child is upset about missing school because he didn't have clean clothes to wear. No one took the time to explain how one might sync lessons together on an iPad or how to run a popcorn machine during the school fundraising event. Yes, I learned how to track a child's fluency and the foundations of reading instruction, but during my first year as a teacher, I quickly realized I had to change my perspective of what the classroom was and adjust with each new group of students I was given.

I QUICKLY REALIZED I HAD TO CHANGE MY PERSPECTIVE OF WHAT THE CLASSROOM WAS AND ADJUST WITH EACH NEW GROUP OF STUDENTS I WAS GIVEN.

As an educator, I believe all students should be able to learn in an environment where they feel safe and loved. Students will work hard for someone they feel is on their side and for someone they can relate to. I believe *every* student can learn, and my job is to identify each student's individual learning needs and objectives and work with him or her to meet them. Students *have* to do school; my job is to show them how *fun* learning can be, so they *want* to learn far beyond the limited time they spend in my classroom. Cultivating creativity and curiosity through collaboration is key and, hopefully, when the year is complete, my students will not only remember the content we covered, but they will also remember that I cared about them and valued each of their unique personalities.

JOE

I want to set the record straight from the start: teaching was *not* my first choice as a profession. Kristin and I may appear similar, but we took very different paths to get to the same point. In fact, I went through a *lot* to get where I am today, but I am grateful for it all because each step taught me a different lesson and made me the person I now am.

High school was a struggle for me—not so much academically, but more so socially. Sure, I had a few core friends, but I had a hard time identifying with the "popular crowd." I wasn't interested in trying to fit in, having an expensive car, or memorizing the words to the hottest song on the radio. I often found myself left out or looking on from the outside. Ultimately, this social difference led me to music. For years, I played music in bands, where I learned the true meaning and importance of being innovative.

Musicians honor this unspoken rule: *Do not take or imitate the creative work of another artist.* As a result, musicians must be original—meaning a lot of work, and at times, frustration. They must learn to work with other strong willed musicians, while at the same time surrounding themselves with others who think like they do. The perfect balance is hard to maintain, but without it the musical machine will not function.

While playing music, I also worked in a local grocery store to help support myself. I spent a lot of time doing "grocery store" tasks—properly stocking shelves, running a cash register, cleaning floors, and unloading a truck. But I also learned how important it was to work together with others. Without this, the job didn't get done, and we all suffered by having to stay late.

Fast forward several years. I was just two credits from graduating with a computer information systems and graphic design degree when I decided this particular career path was not for me. (Ask me sometime about my Comic Sans story!) I had moved away from the grocery store and was now working as an advisor with an after-school program at a local elementary school. Because I had always enjoyed working with kids and wanted to make a difference in the lives of others, I abruptly decided to make a career change. (Don't worry. Kristin was *totally* cool with it! Well … sort of.)

I worked hard to complete my new degree and was fortunate to land my final internship at the same school where Kristin was already employed. I took over for a teacher who was going on leave and not returning. If I played my cards right, this long-term position could potentially become a permanent one. Did I mention this was a fourth-grade position—the same grade and team as Kristin? Yes! I started on the same grade level and team as my wife! I should just say our dinner conversations were rather boring. But, again, I learned the importance of being able to work well with others. Fortunately, I was offered a permanent job, though my principal at the time honored my request to move to a first-grade position—a dream come true for me!

My first year teaching did not go as I had anticipated. I tried to figure out what worked best for the kids in my classroom, and I took resources from anyone and everyone. I listened, learned, and implemented. From there, I tweaked the resources given to me to better fit the needs of my students. Year after year, I used the same baseline resources and kept tweaking them to meet the needs of my current students. Eventually, I was creating most of my classroom resources from scratch, and they were traveling outside of the walls of my classroom, being used by other teachers within my district.

Over time I learned that whether you are a grocery store clerk, a graphic designer, a rock star musician, or a teacher—who is, in reality, grocery store clerk, graphic designer, *and* rock star all in one!—you have to be organized, strategic, collaborative, and consistent to be successful. When you put in effort, you'll be amazed at what you can produce. But you must do your part—and a *lot* of work.

THEMERRILLSEDU

We may have separate classrooms filled with a different sets of students, but we see many of the same trends. Our students live in an era of emojis and six-second videos. "Snaps" are exchanged instead of conversations, and "Alexa" and "Siri" are becoming the newest members of countless classrooms. Our students are expert time savers and can order items from a store to be delivered or picked up at a kiosk. We have noticed that our students view their time as valuable, and they have short attention spans when things don't interest them or aren't important to them. Over time we have learned that our students communicate in small, bite-sized chunks and their primary—and preferred!—mode of communication is no longer text. It is simply images and video. Our students have made clear to us that they don't have time for long-winded explanations *of* things; rather, they want efficient ways *to* communicate information.

"Technology is not going away. Students are not going to abandon devices in their homes. We need to find creative ways to deliver lessons infused with technology. This is how they learn. Actually, this is how we as adults learn, too. When we don't know how to do something, or how to pronounce a new word, we Google it. Why wouldn't we value edtech as teachers?"

—Gloriann Heikes (@MrsHeikes)

This next generation of students learns differently—and must be taught differently. Their brains are uniquely wired, and many attention problems are exacerbated when they are forced into the old traditional model of school. If educators want this generation to be successful in their classrooms, they must figure out who these students are, what they want, and how they communicate.

These students are going to be the driving force behind the next century of innovation. Regardless of the generations to come and what they are being called, educators must understand how these students are learning within their new environments and what external factors are shaping their intelligence. Alongside this knowledge will come an understanding of how educators can better shape their classrooms to accommodate these learners and the ways they think, learn, and communicate in a classroom environment.

One thing is certain: Educators cannot continue teaching in the same structured classrooms, with the same outdated materials, and in the same standardized ways. Innovative learning never stops, and educators need to ensure that their teaching practices keep up, because this next generation's innovative spirit is already being felt. Educators need to adjust. They need to shift their thinking—carefully balancing what is relevant in the eyes of their students and how they can be responsive to this.

ONE THING IS CERTAIN: EDUCATORS CANNOT CONTINUE TEACHING IN THE SAME STRUCTURED CLASSROOMS, WITH THE SAME OUTDATED MATERIALS, AND IN THE SAME STANDARDIZED WAYS.

Throughout this book, we will guide you through the process of transforming your classroom into a truly interactive space. We will also share simple ways to make your lessons more engaging and interactive as well. We will discuss the importance of meaningful relationships with students and their parents and look at how these can be more interactive as well. These easy changes will increase the level of collaboration and interaction between you and your upcoming Gen Z students, giving you the tools needed to truly transform the traditional classroom.

Regardless of the paths we took to where we are now, we have one thing in common: we teach because we care for kids. We go to work every day hoping to make the world a better place. We desire not only to help students master their multiplication tables and properly punctuate a sentence, but we also want to instill in this next generation of students the important skills of empathy, compassion, and problem solving. We want our time with each student to be purposeful and full of meaning. We strive to teach in a way that builds confidence in all learners, while also engaging and motivating them to become the best versions of themselves.

We believe you desire all of these things as well. Maybe you picked up this book looking for new and fresh lesson ideas. Or perhaps you are new to teaching and are looking for guidance in all things "classroom." Now is the best time to start. Find your tribe, and surround yourself with those who inspire you to do things differently. Team up with people who see the need for the same changes you desire—educators who are willing to take risks, think outside the box, and share their ideas for others to use and learn from. Make the commitment to embark on an interACTIVE journey!

GETTING STARTED: UNDERSTANDING INTERACTIVE

CHAPTER 1

INTERACTIVE *ADJECTIVE*
\ ˌin-tər- ˈak-tiv \
ACTING ONE UPON OR WITH THE OTHER

@TheMerrillsEDU

Likely, when you were in school, you studied the brain and learned about its functions. The left side of the brain controls the right side of the body along with logical tasks related to science and mathematics. The right side of the brain controls the left side of the body while helping manage more creative and artistic tasks. Together, both hemispheres work to coordinate emotions, movements, behavior, thoughts, moods, and memory. But beyond the basic structure and functions of the brain, what role does it really play in a person's intelligence?

In a 2006 TedTalk, Sir Ken Robinson said,

> *Intelligence is dynamic. If you look at the interactions of a human brain, intelligence is wonderfully interactive. The brain isn't divided into compartments. In fact, creativity—which I define as the process of having original ideas that have value—more often than not comes about through the interaction of different disciplinary ways of seeing things.*

The brain isn't compartmentalized or as task-specific as people have believed in the past. Although different parts of the brain are responsible for specific functions, they work together simultaneously and, more importantly, in relation with their surroundings.

When sensory information is received, it isn't immediately sent to the left or right hemisphere; rather, it is directed to either the front or the back part of the brain. The front part, or *reflective* brain, handles responsive thinking. This is where you consciously process and reflect on new information. By contrast, the back part of the brain is the *reactive* brain, where you instinctively react to information you receive. When you are relaxed, you control what information your brain stores and what it turns away or keeps out. You have the ability to regulate information when it comes through the responsive, "thinking" brain. As long as you feel safe and are happy, the way your brain works leaves you in complete control.

But how often do you go through a day without feeling anything negative? Likely, not frequently. So it's realistic to expect the same from your students. As negative experiences pile up, they cause the brain to become more and more sensitive. Stress, anger, fatigue, sadness, and feelings of being overwhelmed all can cause the responsive brain to shut down, letting the reactive brain take over. The reactive brain responds in one of three ways: It either ignores, fights, or avoids the sensory information trying to enter the brain.

Ignoring the information means a student's brain shuts down, not allowing information to enter. If the student's brain tries to *fight* the information, it literally sends messages to the body to treat the new information like it would a negative experience, instructing the body to "act out" against the sensory information trying to enter. Have you ever tried to get through a lesson while combating negative behavior or small, disruptive outbursts? Quite possibly one of your students, because of a negative experience or feeling, was being told by her brain to fight off the new information. (And to think all this time you thought she was just being difficult?!) In addition to ignoring and fighting new sensory information, the student's brain also may send signals to *avoid* the information, leading to behaviors such as daydreaming.

When information is routed to the *reactive* brain—regardless of which of the three ways it responds—a student is unlikely to process or remember the information. Educators need to take this information about how the brain responds and use it to create low-stress and high-interest learning environments, lessons, and overall experiences for students. Students are much more likely to retain information gained through these types of experiences in environments like these. Educators want learners who are *responsive*, not reactive.

EDUCATORS WANT LEARNERS WHO ARE RESPONSIVE, NOT REACTIVE.

IMPORTANCE OF INTERACTIVE LEARNING

Educators are responsible for creating the optimal learning environments for their students. Learning needs to be interACTIVE and happen in a way that allows students to be *responsive* rather than reactive. One way you can ensure that your students' learning is interACTIVE is to make sure it is rigorous. *Rigor* is a buzzword in education and is often used to describe extremely thorough and tough learning. Personally, we like to think of rigor as the fine line between an activity a student might perceive as frustrating and one he finds challenging. Rigor is the sweet spot between these two, in which the student is asked to do a task possibly above his independent level but, because he finds it engaging and interactive, he doesn't find it frustrating.

This is why an interACTIVE classroom is so vital for teachers today. Simply assigning the difficult and challenging tasks won't result in optimal learning. Without engagement, students will find the lesson too challenging, become frustrated, and simply send the sensory information over to the reactive brain, where it will be ignored, fought, or avoided. Adding interACTIVE elements to a lesson not only keeps students' brains functioning in a responsive way, but it allows students to learn in a stress-free environment, giving their brains time to process the sensory information in a way that will lead to better overall retention.

It's no coincidence that elements of a rigorous classroom are also elements supporting responsive brain processing. Take a minute to look at some of the differences below.

Rigorous Classroom (Responsive Thinking Environment)	Non-Rigorous Classroom (Reactive Thinking Environment)
Student choice	Boredom
Teachers use music, humor, movement, and novelty	Frustration
	Fear
Actively challenging ideas	No personal relevance found in learning
Gratitude shown	Anxiety over test taking and memorization
Sense of optimism	Feeling of being overwhelmed
	Inability to organize information or responsibilities

All of this sounds good in theory, but the *what* is only half of the interAC-TIVE equation. Educators also need to alter their thinking more in *how* they teach than in *what* they teach. When they change the *how*, their classrooms instantly become more interACTIVE. They need to build an environment in which the diverse needs of students are taken into account and where students feel welcomed and valued. They must have a clear focus on long-term goals and expectations for their students while embedding a substantial space for student voice. Allowing this new generation of students to speak and discover the power in their words will increase interaction and develop their desire to learn in the classroom.

EDUCATORS ALSO NEED TO ALTER THEIR THINKING MORE IN *HOW* THEY TEACH THAN IN *WHAT* THEY TEACH.

"*Collaboration has changed education. Students are now able to interact with the content, their peers and the world in a more authentic way. Not only do students work together, they are practicing real world applications with tools that break down the four walls of their classroom. To truly understand the world is to change it. What better way to understand and engage with the world than to learn from one another and make a difference they can own.*"

—Melinda Hurt (@mrshurtteaches)

BEGINNING YOUR INTERACTIVE JOURNEY

CHAPTER 2

RESPONSIVE *ADJECTIVE*

\ ri-ˈspän(t)-siv \
QUICK TO ACT, ESPECIALLY TO MEET THE NEEDS OF
SOMEONE OR SOMETHING

@TheMerrillsEDU

If this new generation of learners is now sitting in classrooms with troves of information and endless opportunities at their fingertips, what is the role of the teacher? When you think about educating these students and preparing to have them as participants in your classroom, you need to hold tight to your tried and true pedagogy. Dialogue and questioning, higher-order thinking, and metacognition still need to be present within your lessons. You can still make a place for guided learning, individual activities, and structured work all in the same classroom. You don't need to completely throw out the "big book of teaching" or the "guide for learning"; however, you definitely need to update it. Teachers always need to be ready to change and adapt as they see fit.

Almost fifty years ago, child psychologist Jean Piaget said,

> *The principal goal of education is to create men who are capable of doing new things, not simply repeating what other generations have done—men who are creative, inventive, and discoverers.*

Piaget was right. Education should be interactive. The definition of *interactive* is "influencing or having an effect on each other." We want the activities we do with our students to be meaningful and to result in students walking away from our classes with new ideas, skills, and thinking. But in addition to being a place of activity, our classroom also needs to be a place where students see themselves. For something to be interactive, it has to be responsive. Unfortunately, many classrooms today are the exact opposite of responsive. All too often, classrooms are industrialized places where students are asked to conform. They have become places where information is directly delivered to students. High value is often placed on memorization of things like multiplication facts and SAT prep—unfortunately, information is too quickly forgotten after the initial assessment. Students have little time, if any, to reflect on their learning or their specific capabilities as learners. In addition to this, think of *how long* students are forced to conform in this way. They spend roughly seven hours a day, five days a week, working hard just to digest the enormous loads of material being funneled their way. On average, each year, students spend 180 days at school, which amounts to over 1,200 hours within the four walls of a classroom.

In light of this, classrooms should offer specific parameters to help guide and support student learning, giving students a deeper and richer learning experience while empowering them to discover their passions. Teachers need to balance the required standards while giving choice to students. How are you using your 1,200 hours with your students? Are you creating responsive and interactive lessons? Are you giving your students opportunities to speak and use their voices to solve problems and think critically? If the students didn't *have* to come to class, would they miss the time they spend with you?

CLASSROOMS SHOULD OFFER SPECIFIC PARAMETERS TO HELP GUIDE AND SUPPORT STUDENT LEARNING, GIVING STUDENTS A DEEPER AND RICHER LEARNING EXPERIENCE WHILE EMPOWERING THEM TO DISCOVER THEIR PASSIONS.

Your head may be starting to swirl with questions:

- How am I supposed to change everything I have already learned and worked so hard to perfect?

- I don't have enough time as it is now—I certainly don't have time to change things.

Don't become overwhelmed with the uprooting of everything you have known about teaching and learning. Simply cling to one word—*interACTIVE*—and ask yourself a few questions:

- How can I take what I have already created and make room for interaction?
- How can I be more intentional in the interactions I have with students?
- How will my students interact with the content in the classroom?

Take a closer look at some of the ways you can add interaction into the classroom while also becoming more relevant and fostering responsive thinking from students.

STUDENT CHOICE

Giving students choice while also covering standards and keeping the learning in the classroom on track can be done in numerous ways. Student choice can be given and used either in *what* is being learned or in *how* the information is being learned.

When you give students choice over the subjects they want to learn, you are focusing on the *what*. This gives your classroom more of an inquiry-based feel. By strategically scaffolding students, you provide learners with the necessary skills, knowledge, and understanding to be successful in their inquiry while gradually increasing the amount of student agency. Students direct the lessons and drive them based on their interests. Teachers guide learning through questioning and give students real-world problems to solve, leading to higher levels of engagement, with students feeling more connected to the learning process.

You can also focus on the *how* when you give students choice in the way they show mastery of a concept or skill. This model gives the teacher more control over the content in the classroom but gives students choice in how they show their mastery of the skill or

> **Want to learn more?** If you are interested in learning more about implementing choice through inquiry, check out some of these recommended resources:
>
> - *Dive into Inquiry* by Trevor MacKenzie
> - *Inquiry Mindset* by Rebecca Bathurst-Hunt and Trevor MacKenzie
> - *Empower* by John Spencer and A.J. Juliani

> Check out some tools and lesson ideas we have used to foster choice successfully in the classroom.
>
>

standard taught. This option is very popular today, and you may already foster student choice through choice boards and student contracts. When you give students choice, it is important to remember that great scaffolding is needed alongside the choice to ensure students are working productively, without frustration or distraction.

MUSIC

Students respond positively to music—regardless of their talents or interest in it. And they don't all have to like the same kinds of music to experience its many benefits either. Listening to and playing music in the classroom can create a more positive classroom atmosphere and improve learning. It helps the brain process information and enhances the learning environment for all students. You can integrate music into your classroom in a number of ways.

TRANSITIONS—When you play specific songs regularly in the classroom, students learn to regard them as transition signals.

TIMERS—If you choose songs based on length and students listen to them regularly, they learn to judge their time based on the song. Create playlists sorted by length based on how long you want students to work. You can also choose fun music, like the theme melodies from *Jeopardy* or *Looney Toons* to match specific time limits to games.

TEACH CONTENT—Using music to help teach content can be powerful. Connect with students by choosing a song popular *this year* and rewrite the words to match the content you are teaching. Better yet—ask students to show their mastery of content by writing their own song! (Be ready to adjust though! As music trends ebb and flow, you may need to rewrite your song to stay current and relatable with students.)

Are you interested in using music in the classroom but unsure where to start?

Take a look at our top playlists!

MOVEMENT

Closely related to music, getting students up and moving is another great way to foster interaction in your instruction. One of our favorite resources to use with students to get them moving is GoNoodle. GoNoodle believes in getting students up and moving *with purpose* and uses video dance tutorials to teach content through music. Students can practice fluency, be introduced to new content, or simply build community together through fun and silly songs. This is a great resource to use for brain breaks, classroom rewards, and so much more. The best part? It is free!

Using manipulatives in the classroom is another way to get students up and moving. Manipulatives can be loosely defined as anything students touch or hold during the completion of their lesson or activity. You can easily integrate movement within a lesson to enhance interaction with content and curriculum in other ways as well.

 GAMES—Converting well-known games and using them in lessons is an easy way to get students up and moving. Using objects such as jumbo wooden Jenga blocks or inflatable dice not only transforms a lesson into a more gamified atmosphere but gets students out of their seats. Twister is an easy game to convert simply by taping task cards to the mat or creating color-coded problems aligned with the spinner.

 DIGITAL SCOOT—Remember the old task card game of the same name? The activity was played by placing a question card on each student desk in the classroom. To play, students moved around the room, from desk to desk, answering questions or solving math problems as they went. Now you can load up a device screen with activities, surveys, response questions—you name it—and easily turn it into a *digital* Scoot. Simply create a Google slides or PowerPoint project with one task per slide. When students begin working, each computer has one of the slides showing on the screen, and no two computers show the same slide simultaneously. For example, one student's computer shows the first slide, and the next computer is positioned to show the second slide, and so forth. We recommend you create more slide activities than you have students, so no one is waiting on another while working. You can "scoot" students throughout the activity as you choose, but regardless of the specific structure, all students will be up and moving—and engaged—while interacting with classroom content.

TABLEAU—This strategy comes from the literal meaning of its name: *living picture*. During this activity, students create a "frozen" picture to communicate an idea or feeling related to a specific topic or question. Students try to express their thoughts through gestures, physical poses, and facial expressions—but no words! Using this activity is a great way to determine whether students can evaluate information and think critically while working together.

After teaching a concept or reading a selection, ask students to convey meaning by creating a tableau. Students work in groups of two to four to represent the topic you've assigned. Then give students time to brainstorm their ideas and practice their tableau. When time is up, students present their frozen tableau to the class. They each must speak independently and together as a group in a specific, allotted amount of words.

You can easily incorporate tableau into class topics such as:

- representing the most important scene from a story
- depicting *Would You Rather* scenarios
- summarizing an event in history
- imagining what would happen if…
- identifying details from the text to support
- portraying famous or historical people and their actions

HUMOR

Laughter really is the best medicine. Laughing lowers your blood pressure, reduces stress, and produces an overall general sense of wellbeing. Some say laughter adds years to your life. Being able to laugh at a situation or a mistake is a valuable skill to model and teach to your students. If you can create and foster an environment in which mistakes are valuable learning moments— rather than humiliating and embarrassing ones—students will naturally become more responsive learners.

You can integrate humor in your interactions with students *and* through your lessons. Integrating funny sayings such as "Come on, man!" from ESPN's blooper segment is an easy way to show students that mistakes are okay and should be brushed off and learned from. Creative lessons like this one also integrate humor through the academic standard theme.

NOVELTY

Students are always talking about new songs on the radio, new shows on television, and new famous personalities. Teachers should capitalize on these novel things their students enjoy and use them to foster engagement. As we mentioned earlier, you might write new lyrics to a current popular song to help teach your weekly science concept. Or perhaps you use the latest video game trend to gamify a lesson in which students can "power up" as they work. Using objects your students are interested in instantly makes you more relevant in their eyes.

Newsela is a great online resource we use when looking for current reading material. Its goal is to foster student engagement through fresh, adaptive reads for every student. Newsela's database houses articles rooted in history, infused with math, or on the tail of current events. You can even level readings for different ability groups, and most articles come with questions and correlated writing tasks. It's a great resource to use when building lessons relevant to student interests. And the base version is free!

Let's face it, in today's day and age, technology easily becomes a novelty and of great interest to our students. Try building lessons in which they show their learning through the eyes of a social media app. Analyzing a character from a novel? Why not create an Instagram profile for them? Want students to infer dialog between two famous historical figures? Maybe students could create a curation of text message conversations between the two. Make note of how your students interact with various lessons and use this to identify what they're most interested in, and then select similar but fresh content to keep student engagement high. Included below are some great resources from educators; you can get templates to start your lessons!

**Use the QR Code to download
the app texting story!**

THE #INTERACTIVE CLASS @THEMERRILLSEDU

USE THIS SPACE FOR SKETCH NOTES, IDEAS, ETC!

THE INTERACTIVE TEACHING METHOD

CHAPTER 3

METHOD *NOUN*

\ ˈme-thəd \

A PROCEDURE, TECHNIQUE, OR WAY OF DOING SOMETHING, ESPECIALLY IN ACCORDANCE WITH A DEFINITE PLAN

@TheMerrillsEDU

Students do not learn in the same way we did when we were in school. Yet educators continually try to reinvent new ways to teach students based on the *old* ways they are familiar with—in which students learn best when they *sit* and *listen* to their teacher, *behave* well, and *practice* the same skills over and over. This can lead to educators comparing traditional teaching methods with more modern ones and, in doing so, finding themselves divided over where they should fall on the continuum of effective teaching practices.

We want to avoid the debate over the pros and cons of technology versus the benefits of using pencil and paper. Our goal in this book is to focus on the things we have tried and implemented in our classrooms and our personal experiences leading to successful and interACTIVE teaching and learning with students.

Although negative behaviors can impede learning, the way educators teach should not be influenced by the behavior they *see*. Fun activities, instructional technology, and cooperative games should be fundamental elements and integral tools found in all aspects of teaching and learning—not simply rewards given to students who have behaved well or finished all their work. Teaching should always be composed of the same elements regardless of students' behaviors. All students can learn. In fact, we have found that the more teachers transition their classrooms along the engagement spectrum, the more the negative, disrupting behaviors slowly begin to disappear and disintegrate. Why? Because learning becomes more real and authentic—and fun!

THE WAY EDUCATORS TEACH SHOULD NOT BE INFLUENCED BY THE BEHAVIOR THEY *SEE*.

Just as the role of the learner has changed, so has the role of the teacher. Teachers don't need others to relay information to them—and neither do their students. In many cases, students don't even need the help of their parents to obtain information. With a simple Google search, Siri question, or hashtag hunt, our students can learn about anything they want and travel to any place they choose. How do educators teach a generation already proficient with accessing information?

If teachers are truly building lessons tailored to the needs of students in their current classrooms, then the traditional model of teaching is no longer effective. Educators must switch the way they develop and plan their lessons so they inherently become less teacher-centered and more student-centered. This shift comes when educators adopt a truly interactive method for teaching and learning in the classroom.

> *"I value edtech because it keeps me on my toes to see what's new and improved and how it can best be used to better engage students so they see their learning as fresh and relevant to their interests."*
>
> —Jennifer Saarinen (@snej80)

DEVELOPING THE INTERACTIVE CLASSROOM

As you begin your journey into the interACTIVE classroom, be assured it's a process—not a trip you make in a single leap. It is not something you will master quickly or even be great at right away. As with anything, the more practice and explicit attention you give to changing your approach to teaching, the more seamless you will become with it. The interACTIVE method is comprised of five parts and is designed to help you PIVOT your traditional classroom into one that is more engaging and interACTIVE.

Interactive Method:
Prepare → Innovate → Visualize → Observe → Troubleshoot

PREPARE—As a teacher, you need to prepare your own interACTIVE learning environment. This environment and the lessons found within it do not happen overnight. Rather, it will occur with intentional planning and preparation. This preparation may actually include getting rid of things you currently use—structures, physical items, or curricula—modeled after the traditional classroom. You need to prepare your classroom for collaborative and cooperative work and create specific spaces designed for student-centered learning. Consider and prepare to meet the specific needs of your students. Make learning tools available and easily accessible for them to use as they choose. Integrate opportunities for autonomy and for students to explore and share their interests in your interACTIVE classroom.

INNOVATE—The ability to create is one of the most powerful privileges you have as a teacher. You are in charge of creating an inviting—but also functional—classroom environment. Every part of your day should be planned and tailored to the students learning in your classroom—from seating arrangements to lesson content and activity structures, and *more*. Your lessons should always be improving, and no two should ever look alike. You can build innovative experiences for your students by gathering and creating materials rather than simply using what is laid out in a textbook and workbook combination. You can incorporate text sets, HyperDocs, unit studies, and so much more! You are tasked with creating a balanced classroom where structure and student autonomy coexist. Your goal is to give students responsibility and choice in their learning environment and lessons, while also guiding them through the implementation and monitoring the structure.

VISUALIZE—Before launching a lesson with your students, take time to visually and mentally plan it out. For best results, take into account even the smallest aspects of your lessons to ensure they run the way you envision them. We advise writing down your intentions, because we have learned over time that the lessons we planned out ran better. The structure and form of your planning can vary, and we are not here to tell you what the structure needs to look like or even what it needs to include (a lot of this will vary and often will be determined by your school district or administration).

Regardless of the format you choose, we do recommend you ask yourselves several questions we always ask ourselves when planning a new and innovative lesson to ensure we stay on track:

- Where will students be seated and how does this facilitate the activity?
- Will students be up and moving?
- How will I engage my students' interests while covering the necessary content?
- Will students have time to collaborate and talk with their classmates?
- How long will each activity realistically take?
- What role will I play throughout this lesson?
- Did I include a chance for my students to revise knowledge before the lesson ends?
- How do I make this lesson authentic? Will students have a chance to share their learning with others?

OBSERVE—Although you will naturally be a part of your interACTIVE lesson, your role as a teacher is to observe. In relation to what you had expected, what are students saying, doing, and possibly feeling while they work? Reflect on these observations. Did the lesson allow students the freedom intended? Did something about the lesson cause an unexpected struggle or interruption? Did the lesson allow students to gain an understanding of the material needed to move on to the next part of the lesson? Is any remediation needed?

Reflecting naturally leads you back to preparing a new lesson based on what you observed. You may possibly revise and modify lessons already launched or prepare for upcoming lessons based on the successes you just had. Either way, reflection is a vital part of the interACTIVE learning process. True growth will never come unless reflection is included in the creative process.

TROUBLESHOOT—Many benefits come when you hand over the reins to your students and start building and carrying out more interactive and student-centered lessons. Students will be more engaged. They will start taking ownership of their learning and focusing more on the quality of their work. Creativity will grow and spark new learning that was not necessarily noted on the lesson plan.

Be aware—Accompanying all of these benefits is *struggle*. Guaranteed. Transforming the way you think, create, and teach is not as simple as it sounds. It will be hard at times. You, just like your Gen Z students, live in an age of instant gratification. You can be influenced by photos and videos on social media, peruse how-to tutorials, and link resources with your work. You can read blogs and "pin" ideas you want to come back to later. You can even go to websites and, for a few dollars, buy a ready-made lesson to print or a door decoration ready to hang!

Even educators can easily forget the special kind of learning gained through the struggle of persisting through a problem. Through these struggles you learn about yourself. You learn about standards. You even learn about your students! If you find part of a lesson you don't like—pivot! Change things up as you go, or revisit part of the process to make sure your students leave with the understanding of the content you originally visualized them gaining.

EVEN EDUCATORS CAN EASILY FORGET THE SPECIAL KIND OF LEARNING GAINED THROUGH THE STRUGGLE OF PERSISTING THROUGH A PROBLEM.

In a perfect world, you would prepare, innovate, visualize, observe, and troubleshoot every time you prepare a lesson or unit—and repeat this "no fail" process over and over. Then, magically, your classroom would transform into self-regulating, innovatively interactive places where learning reaches its truest form! Sorry to break it to you—this educational Utopia doesn't exist. In fact, often this process looks more like a ball of yarn than a simple, linear process. You may master the model, but you will find yourself going back to various steps in no specific order, depending on your students' needs and unexpected challenges and circumstances. For example, a school assembly is scheduled smack dab in the middle of your instructional block! You have to pivot back and rework! Maybe a student has a sudden death in the family and comes to school in no shape to focus and learn. You simply pivot and try again! You visualized using a new technology and wind up with nothing but technical difficulties. *Pivot*! Don't be afraid of making a mistake or messing up. Embrace those opportunities!

> "Be okay with things not going perfectly the first time and lean on some of the most helpful people in the room, the students!"
>
> —Michael Drezek (@M_drez)

Defining the interACTIVE method of teaching is just the start to developing an interACTIVE class. You definitely need to understand and acknowledge the elements you want to build your lessons or classroom environment around. The cycle of preparing, innovating, visualizing, observing, and troubleshooting will continue to revolve—and evolve—as you acquire new skills, more modern learning tools, and improved ways to teach this new generation of learners.

But how do teachers develop and incorporate these interACTIVE ideals in a consistent, natural, and effortless way? They do it through grit and growth.

GRIT AND GROWTH

Grit is a well-known word currently garnering a lot of attention in the educational community. Coined by psychologist and researcher Angela Duckworth, the term is defined as the "combination of passion and perseverance needed to achieve some form of long-term goal." Just as with any goal-setting, your success will be determined by your individual ability to stay focused and on track. This requires discipline, determination, and courage. Many of the qualities educators teach their kids when referring to grit and goal-setting are just as applicable to themselves.

Developing an interACTIVE class isn't for the faint of heart. It doesn't happen overnight. Nor is it an easy "one size fits all" approach you can simply purchase online. The interACTIVE class isn't achieved by developing great new lessons, only to reuse them year after year. Creating a relevant and responsive classroom requires resolve and determination. Preparing and creating new and innovative lessons calls for patience and discipline. You need this focus as you persist through the rough patches, optimistically reflecting on all of the variables you could choose to change the next time around. The ultimate goal in this is *growth*—in regard to both student learning and teacher mindset.

Growth, acquired over time, is another concept humans created to help manage, compare, and evaluate. Growth is usually measured in quantitative amounts—money, height, numbers—as a way to compare something current with what came before. Educators refer to growth as the academic progress a student makes. Teachers look to see students evolve from where they were when they started at point A to where they are when they arrive at point B. The only problem is that they also do this by reverting back to society's concept of measuring growth in quantitative measures with tools such as value-added model (VAM) scores, reading levels, test scores, grade point averages, gains, and books read. The list could go on and on. Everything educators use to measure student success uses a number. If teachers can't compare or evaluate it against a standard norm, the traditional way of teaching advises them to avoid using it.

> *"Creativity is the new currency. The world is changing faster than ever in terms of technological advancements. The one thing that will always be in demand is creativity. There is no standardized test for this."*
>
> —Christine McKee (@CMcKee27)

Educators can't develop and make change in their classrooms until they are able to develop meaning beyond these basic numbers. Lessons become transformed when teachers can break free from what they *expect* and start focusing on what they *hope* for. Growth can be shown in many different ways and, although progress monitoring and scale scores still have a place, they should not drive instruction. Freedom and flexibility should be at the forefront as you prepare your classroom for the most recent generation of learners.

EDUCATORS CAN'T DEVELOP AND MAKE CHANGE IN THEIR CLASSROOMS UNTIL THEY ARE ABLE TO DEVELOP MEANING BEYOND THESE BASIC NUMBERS.

Before you start running down the road of change, enthusiastically waving your arms above your head, emphatically yelling about the interACTIVE class to all who will listen, be prepared. Whenever there is change, there is challenge. This intersection is where grit and growth meet. To create this interACTIVE and transformative learning environment, you must be able to persist and persevere through all the potholes, driving with passion for your students and their learning potential. You need to have thick skin when those who disapprove of your ideas cause you to start doubting the meaningfulness of your methods.

WHENEVER THERE IS CHANGE, THERE IS CHALLENGE. THIS INTERSECTION IS WHERE GRIT AND GROWTH MEET.

Transforming how students learn can be a shock to the students themselves. It will take time for them to strengthen their nonquantitative skills such as teamwork, time management, and creativity—skills they were unable to develop in their past, more traditionally structured classrooms. You will be frustrated and feel like a failure. At times you may even feel despair and start to doubt why you turned down this path to begin with. Resist the urge to pull over. If you can persevere in the name of the passion, student growth will follow.

In a truly interACTIVE classroom, you will always have frustrations, mistakes, and lessons to be learned. However, the passion, independence, and confidence created in the midst of it all will fuel your journey and continue to make it well worth the drive.

PEEK INTO AN INTERACTIVE CLASS

CHAPTER 4

ENVIRONMENT *NOUN*

\ *in-ˈvī-rə(n)-mənt* \
THE AGGREGATE OF SURROUNDING THINGS, CONDITIONS, OR INFLUENCES; THE SOCIAL AND CULTURAL FORCES THAT SHAPE THE LIFE OF A PERSON OR A POPULATION

@TheMerrillsEDU

Have you ever thought about your students being shaped both culturally and socially in your classroom space? And shaped—not through your lessons—but through the actual classroom arrangement? Previously, we had not thought of this either, but we have learned this is the essence of an interACTIVE classroom. It is a positive space, designed so students can work toward the goals and objectives set for them by their teacher.

As such, setting up a classroom is now one of the most important things we do at the start of every year. The classroom layout, look, and overall feel will all influence and shape student learning. This does *not* mean you need to buy and stock your room with an enormous amount of new things. But it *does* mean that each and every year you should be making purposeful choices about how you're going to house your new group of students.

Maybe you are at the point where you have an empty classroom stacked with furniture—and no idea where it will end up. You have a mix of school-owned furniture, items you have collected over the years, and hand-me-downs and donations from other teachers. Added to the mix are books, baskets, bins, activity books, and craft supplies. The list could go on and on. With so much "stuff," it is easy to get carried away and create a space that resembles a carnival more than it does a classroom. Environments like this can be overwhelming and overstimulating for students. When you design and decorate, keep these questions in mind as you add each unique element to your space:

- Will this help my students learn?
- Will this space appeal to the various learning needs of my students?
- Will this element help them work?
- Will this be something students can touch, use, or create with while learning?

InterACTIVE classrooms alone are valuable, but they are especially successful when they go hand in hand with a change in pedagogy. The difference for students is not the actual furniture you put in your room—the comfy couch centered facing the board, the ergonomic stools, or the bike pedals under the desks. Rather, the difference is made by how you and your students use the space together to learn. Ultimately, the goal is to create a welcoming and inviting space for all who enter—an ideal space fostering creativity and collaboration among those within.

CHARACTERISTICS OF THE INTERACTIVE CLASS

Teachers often view the classroom as "their space"—the one place they use to define themselves. When others try to tell them what they need to display on the walls or how specific furniture should be set up, they don't often take well to the suggestions. They believe the space within those four walls is theirs, and they want to set it up to function in the best possible way for *them*.

But is the classroom really theirs? Does it really belong to them? We would venture to say, "No, it doesn't." The classroom serves as a space for students, a place they can come to inquire, learn, and grow, and an environment offering students choice to encourage and enhance their learning. Regardless of the combination you use, keeping your classroom focused on student choice helps you create a meaningful learning environment in which student voice matters.

All classrooms—no matter the size or shape of the space—should be designed with this goal in mind and with the same simple qualities. FACE it—with so many different ideas and themes, and you can easily become overwhelmed or get a bit carried away. Setting up a classroom can be a lot easier if you adhere to our basic "FACE" framework. An interactive classroom should be *flexible, authentic, colorful,* and *engaging.*

FLEXIBLE

No two students are alike, and the way they learn is just as different, so flexibility needs to be the first quality of a truly interACTIVE classroom. Flexibility means something is easily modified and willing to change or compromise. When an object is flexible, it can bend easily without breaking. When you design your classroom space to change based on who occupies it and what tasks are being completed there, you are adding flexibility. A flexible classroom inherently gives students choice within the space.

As you set up a flexible classroom, think about the physical space itself *and* the tools used within it. No two classrooms are alike when it comes to physical space and layout. Some are large and spacious; others are small, cramped, and tight. One room may be lined with windows while the room next to it is dark with bare walls. Regardless of the size and shape of your room, you can create a *flexible* interactive space. When you do, a fluidity will take over the space and transform it. Rather than one large learning space, you will now have numerous smaller areas where learning can occur. Gone are traditional beliefs such as: the teacher's reading table is only for the teacher and her small group, the desks are where students learn, and the carpet is the class's meeting spot. Instead, the classroom has been transformed to include a large spacious table with stools where students can sit and work cooperatively. Tables or desks with chairs are available for students to work independently on an assignment with a partner. Now, in addition to serving as a class meeting space, the large carpet is a place where students can "choose" to sit on the floor and spread out while working. Often the "front" of the room disappears because there are numerous focal points and places where the class can meet and from which you can deliver content.

As you design your flexible classroom and the different learning spaces to sprinkle throughout the space, keep these aspects in mind:

WHOLE-CLASS MEETING SPACE—You should have at least one large space where the class can gather for whole group instruction. This can be on a carpet on the floor or in groups of desks or large tables. Simply put, is there a place where everyone can sit together and be addressed at the same time? Don't be afraid to move away from desks. Clipboards or small whiteboards provide an easy way for students to write while allowing them to be all together in one space.

SMALL GROUP WORKSPACE—Smaller spaces where students can work alone or in small groups or pairs should be sprinkled throughout the learning environment. These can be an oddly shaped nook in the corner, a wall under a ledge, or even a space designated by a specific area rug or carpet. Something as small as a group of pillows in a corner can be inviting for students and signal a place to work together.

FLEXIBLE SEATING—Once you have your learning spaces spread out and designated, you have to think about seating. Try to vary the types of seating choices available to students—stools, chairs, benches, beach chairs—because what works for one student may not work for another. The type of seating also may differ depending on the space. Long counters give space for stools, and empty corners are more inviting for pillows or floor seating. Consider giving a survey after the first few weeks of school to get the students' input! They are the ones who must use the space for learning and will be able to give the best feedback.

AUTHENTIC

Making learning authentic allows students to "learn by doing" instead of simply acquiring and retaining information. When learning is authentic, students naturally have more buy-in and are more engaged. Your physical classroom is no different than your lessons when it comes to authenticity. As you begin designing your learning space, think about how students are going to become comfortable and connect with the space. Teachers spend hours setting up their classrooms hoping to land on the most perfect arrangement so students will instantly feel at home. Ironically, this is usually done before they ever meet a single student—before they learn their names. Everything is set up before students introduce themselves to each other and before the teacher has a chance to learn about them and what they are interested in.

This doesn't mean you need to do nothing all summer, only to spend your first week of school with students moving around furniture and decorating the walls with motivational quotes. But it does mean to keep a few things in mind when creating an authentic space for your students:

MAKE THE ROOM RELEVANT—Leave at least fifty percent of your classroom wall space empty. If you have bulletin boards, you may want to cover them but not post anything on them. Allow them to wait for students' work and ideas to be hung on them. Leaving space "untouched" gives your students a place to fill buckets, brainstorm ideas, or share book reviews. You might use a free space to post login steps for a program they are having trouble remembering. Every day, students will generate ideas and ways to learn and share with each other. Having the extra space to say "Yes!" to an original idea can make all the difference to students. They will feel like they have a space for their contributions—one meeting their specific needs and goals.

CREATE AN INTERACTIVE AND EVER-CHANGING SPACE—In our classrooms, we do this with a bulletin board dedicated to student art and written thoughts. It is a place where students are allowed to post their work freely and where materials can be taken down at any time. Through the years, students have created personal artwork to give as an end of year present to hang proudly for the next class to admire. For some students, this may be the only safe space they have to share their thoughts and feelings with others. It becomes a place where their voice is valued, and they have choice as to when and how they share.

COLORFUL

Research has shown that engaging classrooms improve student learning, and color is one of the most common ways teachers achieve this engagement. Think about it: Color has been used to attract students' attention since the first schoolhouse was painted red. Recently, thanks to the internet, the practice of adding color has begun to spiral a bit out of control. Through social media and online avenues such as Pinterest, Instagram, and Teachers Pay Teachers, educators can share (and sell!) their ideas like never before. But beware! This abundance of resources can quickly overload a space and become distracting. Keep your students and their best interests at heart when designing. Ask yourself, "Am I designing for learning or decorating for looks?" As we mentioned previously, teachers want to create an interactive learning environment in which all elements are placed inside the classroom with the intent to foster student learning and development.

When you use color in the classroom, think about its overall purpose. Are you placing color to help with some sort of organization? Are you integrating color to add to the overall feeling of the space and to make it seem more cohesive? In our case, we often use color differently based on the age level of the students we teach.

In a classroom for pre-kindergarten through second grade students, color is mainly used for classroom management. Colors can represent noise levels or assigned seats on the carpet. They can indicate behavior incentives and easily organize reading groups. Classroom jobs, rules listed on the wall, and even the alphabet are usually multicolored. Colors are one of the first things kids learn when they are younger, and they provide a clear and comfortable way to integrate order into a classroom.

Go a step further than using color just for organization. Try using it to deliver content. Can you use color to help differentiate material? A great time to do this is during reading centers or independent work time. You can place colored stickers or dots on the books in a basket you've chosen for the students to read to help students identify them. You could stack colored folders in a bin to designate the math challenge geared for each group of students. You could even print assignments on the selected color paper to ease organization. Students will become accustomed to looking for the color assigned to them at the given time and will be able to complete assignments more independently. Using various colors is beneficial because a student's color can be changed at any time, allowing for flexibility within the organizational structure.

In an intermediate elementary (third through fifth grades), middle school, or even high school classroom, color can be used to sort or organize students and materials. You may apply many of the strategies for using color to your specific classroom or set of students. But often, as the age of your students increases, they take on more responsibility, including more choice, and the need to use color as an organizational tool tends to decrease.

So naturally, for an intermediate teacher, color becomes a way to create a calm and cohesive space. When you choose colors for the classroom, think about your own home and what you want to be surrounded by for most of the day. Are you choosing and filling the room with colors complimentary to each other? Do the colors overwhelm the space and make it look cluttered or smaller than it really is? Make sure to keep the functions of the colors purposeful. Do they call attention to a specific title or space? Do the colors help students find information or possibly induce a sense of calm and cohesiveness? If the color becomes distracting or intrusive, it has lost its instructional value.

ENGAGING

Teachers often talk about ways to engage students in their lessons, but have you considered how you can use the external environment to foster engagement? The ceiling, floor, and four walls are also important to think about when you design the layout of your classroom. Everything in the classroom should have purpose in engaging students with content, and often this can be done in small, creative ways not requiring a lot of time and money.

PAINTED CEILING TILES—How often do you catch unengaged students staring at the ceiling? Instead of making remarks about them counting the tiles or spaces on the ceiling, what if you could now make looking at the ceiling more meaningful and engaging? Wall space in a classroom is often deemed prime real estate, and by the time mid-year rolls around, the anchor charts and student work have taken over any free space (not to mention the space taken up by numerous fire code rules and regulations). Why not take the learning upwards by painting the tiles? Use the ceiling tiles to paint encouraging quotes to promote kindness, self-advocacy, and grit.

Or take it one step further and paint the things you want to remind students of from past lessons. *Area* versus *perimeter*, various meanings of prefixes and suffixes, or Spanish verb translations could all be used on tiles. The tiles can be used to reinforce concepts and ideas students struggle with or they can restate information often misunderstood. Then, when students look up at the ceiling, they are inspired and engaged—not bored! (And even if they do look up out of boredom, at least they'll be faced with more learning!)

If you want to paint your own tiles, consider these ideas to get you started:

- Area versus perimeter
- Unit conversions
- Measurement concepts (inches/centimeters)
- 2D and 3D shapes
- Types of lines (parallel and perpendicular)
- Types of angles (acute, right, obtuse)
- Place value
- Prefixes and suffixes
- Meaning of *theme*, *main idea*, *figurative language*, or other literary elements
- Misused words such as *there*, *their*, and *they're*
- Tips for paragraph writing
- Presidents
- Book covers from a class read-aloud
- Temperature conversion from Celsius to Fahrenheit
- Pushes versus pulls
- Law of gravity
- Parts of an atom
- Basic world map with the seven continents
- Famous or inspirational quotes
- Hotline numbers for social or emotional resources
- Book cover murals
- Countries and continents
- Historical timeline

 Tip: Most likely in primary grades the tiles will be painted by the classroom teachers or staff and used primarily to engage students with content. However, if you teach older students, such as middle or high school, try using tiles also for motivation by allowing students to collaborate and make a tile summarizing the unit just studied! Or try it out as an end-of-the-year celebration of knowledge!

GREEN SCREEN WALL—The use of video has evolved during the past ten years and is becoming one of the prime ways students take in information today. Why not make it one of the major ways they present what they've learned as well? You can make DIY green screens in many ways, and one of the easiest is to use a wall already in your classroom! By painting a small portion of one of your walls, you now have a permanent place for students to use for video recording, available to use instantly at any moment.

No wall space available? No worries. Try repurposing an old pull-down map or an unused overhead projector screen—those rolls mounted above your front board, covered in dust because they haven't been used in ages? Simply pull down the screen, paint, and allow to dry. Voila! You now have a green screen wall, appearing at the pull of string and staying hidden when not in use. This is a great alternative to painting a wall, especially if your administrators are harder to win over.

Looking for a less permanent green screen? One alternative is plastic tablecloths from the local party store. They usually cost around $1.00 and are easy to tape to any classroom or hallway wall. They can be used and then thrown awayv or saved for another time. Another reusable option is painted trifold boards. Choose the size of board you like and, instead of painting a wall green, just paint the board. You will need to add several coats of paint to the board because of the cardboard's tendency to soak up the paint, but once it's dry, you have a more permanent—yet portable—green screen.

Tip: Teachers have reported using the following colors to great success:

- Behr Disney Gamma Sector Green (Home Depot)
- Neon Green (Sherwin-Williams)
- Valspar 6010-7 Luscious Green (Lowe's Home Improvement)
- Dulux Colour Chroma Key Green

REMOVABLE WALL STICKERS—Removable wall stickers are no longer just a decoration option for a child's bedroom; they also make your classroom environment more engaging. Take your pick from motivational quotes, world maps, or thematic images to adorn the walls of the class. Removable stickers are great because they adhere nicely to all types of surfaces but are as easy to remove as they are to put on. For teachers who are unable to paint for some reason, they offer another way to foster engagement. Can't find the sticker you want? Make your own! Vinyl used for commercial machines like Cricut and Silhouette can be cut and used to create engaging elements too! They are easy to design, cut, and stick on any surface, and come off rather easily if you wish for them to be temporary.

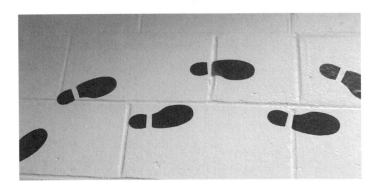

UNCONVENTIONAL CLASSROOM FURNITURE AND ITEMS—In every school district someone in a remote office—far away from any classroom—is responsible for creating the list of items considered to be "standard furniture" for every classroom. This list generally consists of desks, chairs, a whiteboard, possibly a bookcase or two, and maybe a large rug—if you're lucky. This *status quo* furniture is designed to support *status quo* teaching. To change this situation and foster new levels of engagement and learning inside the classroom, a mini makeover may be in order! You can bring many unique pieces of furniture into the classroom to instantly impact student learning.

CLASSROOM STAGE—Using a stage is an inexpensive (and easily movable) way to get your students excited to share in class. You can build one in many ways, and the exact dimensions aren't important. Stages can be built with pallets or plywood, and they instantly communi-

cate that sharing knowledge is worth showing off. Performing on a stage and entertaining the audience helps students engage in their learning—and what is more fun than entertaining other students from atop their own private platform?! In addition to providing a platform for sharing, a stage is a great space for students to work, and it can double as a small group sitting area. If you are crafty enough, you can even create stages with hinged tops to create instant extra storage!

RECORDING BOOTHS AND TENTS—As you discuss and develop places for students to collaborate and work together, don't forget about your more introverted students. Provide quiet, secluded spaces where they can record their work in confidence. Recording booths or simple child tents are great places to do this.

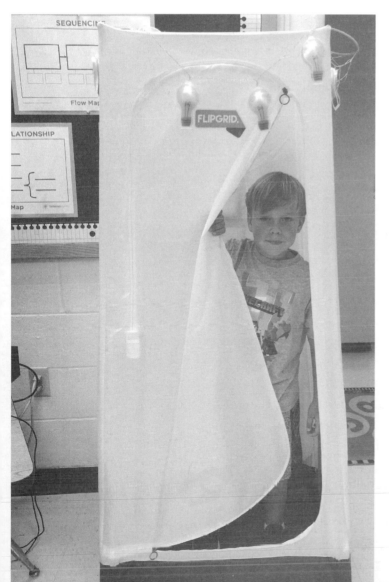

Getting to work inside a tent instantly engages students—regardless of whether they enjoy sharing their ideas with others. These booths or tents are great for large and small spaces because they can be easily taken down, tucked away in a cabinet, or transported to another classroom.

CLASS DOORBELL—It's no secret that sounds help engage students. Chimes, chants, clapping, and countdowns are all great ways to quickly garner students' attention. But what about finding a way to take something normally used outside of the classroom and use it *inside* the learning environment? When you do this, you create instant engagement! Teaching students to go from one activity to the next with minimal interruption is not easy. Plug-in doorbells are an inexpensive way to manage these transitions. Most doorbells play between ten and twenty seconds, providing an opportune amount of time for students to get from point A to point B. This can preserve precious instructional time—*and* add flair to your class. You can even change the chime to match a specific holiday!

ALEXA—Teachers always enjoy announcing a new student is joining the class—especially when she is one who will never speak out of turn or get out of her seat. Alexa is this perfect student! Whether you are working on writing, math, reading, or science, Alexa can participate in it all. Gone are the days when students ask you for help with spelling. When a student finishes his writing early, have no fear! Underline a few words and have him ask Alexa for some better synonyms to use. Maybe Alexa can help skip count in math or be part of the morning meeting and give the weather for the day. She can also divide kids into groups or choose an answer by rolling a dice. There are countless ways to integrate her into the classroom for instant and easy engagement. Consider involving her with these common classroom commands:

- Alexa, what is the definition of…?
- Alexa, what is __ + __? (or any function)
- Alexa, what is a synonym for ___?
- Alexa, what is the weather today?
- Alexa, how do you spell…?
- Alexa, pick a number between __ and __.
- Alexa, roll the dice.
- Alexa, set a timer for…
- Alexa, count by…
- Alexa, tell me a story

THE IMPORTANCE OF HAVING AN INTERACTIVE CLASS

An interACTIVE classroom is a place where students are engaged and challenged. Engagement occurs when students have a relationship with their school, teacher, peers, or classroom curriculum. If educators are not meeting students' academic *and* social-emotional needs, the learning they do in the classroom will be limited. A child won't learn from someone she can't trust or from someone she doesn't like. The relationships you build with your students enable them to "buy in" to your lessons and take risks with their learning. In addition to being engaged cognitively, students can also be engaged both emotionally and behaviorally.

As students engage with interactive learning, they benefit in many ways. In addition to earning better test scores, students who are engaged attend school more regularly and put more effort into their schoolwork. They tend to have better behavior and feel positive about their education. Engaged students are motivated and more willing to take on tasks involving high critical thinking, learning to work and think effectively. Creating an engaging classroom environment is one of the first steps you can take toward creating an interACTIVE experience for your students.

THE #INTERACTIVE CLASS @THEMERRILLSEDU

USE THIS SPACE FOR SKETCH NOTES, IDEAS, ETC!

EMPOWERING STUDENTS IN THE INTERACTIVE CLASS

CHAPTER 5

EMPOWER *VERB*

\ im-ˈpau̇(-ə)r \

TO GIVE POWER OR AUTHORITY TO SOMEONE OR SOMETHING

@TheMerrillsEDU

Teachers can design, develop, and begin creating an interACTIVE classroom, but they must not overlook the importance of the personal relationships they can cultivate with their students at the same time. Engagement is built on relationships, and the most important relationship in the classroom is the one between the teacher and the students. It is safe to say the influence of a teacher may be the most central and impactful thing when predicting the success of a child. As the primary instructor in the room, you are responsible for setting the tone for your students, and you should not take this task lightly.

IT IS SAFE TO SAY THE INFLUENCE OF A TEACHER MAY BE THE MOST CENTRAL AND IMPACTFUL THING WHEN PREDICTING THE SUCCESS OF A CHILD.

Many things teachers do can have a direct and positive impact on student engagement and help develop deeper relationships with their students. For starters, you need to enjoy what you do and let your confidence exude to your students. Students need to come to class every day and find you excited about what you are going to teach and confident you will be able to help them master the chosen content. If you are not excited to be teaching, how can you expect your students to be excited participants and desire to receive your instruction? Students feed off the energy you give out. What kind of vibes are you giving off?

Your desire and drive to improve your methods and personal teaching practices will also help foster deeper and more meaningful student relationships. How are you growing as a teacher? Are you making efforts to stay in touch with youth? Teachers need to stay current and should constantly update their lesson plan playbooks to include more relevant teaching strategies to strengthen their overall practice. You need to stay positive and proactive and continually be on the lookout for new ways to deliver content to your students. This may be easier to do when you have children at home because you are naturally exposed to what is relevant and popular to kids. But as your personal children or grandchildren grow up, your ability to relate is directly correlated and pigeonholed to their ages and interests, and suddenly you're in the same sticky situation of having to stay relevant with the children you teach. You may *think* you're staying relevant and not realize you've really become out of touch. If you're in this situation—or if you're an educator who is not a parent or grandparent—how are you actively staying up to date? Actively seek professional development opportunities and look for new ways to update your teaching practices.

> *"Have the kids learn right along with you. They are such good helpers and can figure things out with you! Let students create and share their voice and your classroom will be an empowering place."*
>
> —Sara Frater (@sarafrater)

Finally, your personal reactions to things can also develop and foster student relationships. You can choose to react to your students and approach your teaching methods in one of two ways: cognitively or emotionally. It's easy for new teachers to get buried beneath rules and procedures and thus think cognitively—focusing simply on checking off all of their tasks for each given day.

As you create and develop relationships with students in the interACTIVE classroom, your methods will likely involve or express more emotion. Connecting with students emotionally, rather than just cognitively, positively impacts your ability to teach students. This connection will help you identify frustrations in students before they even voice them. It will help you gauge the type of day they are having as soon as they walk in the door. Inadvertently, you will become a more consistent listener to your students, enabling you to revise lessons based on their feedback. As you move further away from the cognitive, you will more clearly see the positive influence of an emotional approach on teaching and learning.

CONNECTING WITH STUDENTS EMOTIONALLY, RATHER THAN JUST COGNITIVELY, POSITIVELY IMPACTS YOUR ABILITY TO TEACH STUDENTS.

Once you are able to see the connection between your relationships with students and their engagement in the classroom, you can then focus on *how* to develop and nourish these relationships throughout the school year. When you focus on interactive relationships with students, you need to be *personal*, *positive*, and *proactive*.

> *"It's never about the technology. Technology has the potential to impact and support learning. Tech without impact is just tech. It's the match in a fire. It's the spotlight on a field. It can be the thing to inspire."*
>
> —Amy Storer (@techamys)

MAKE IT PERSONAL

Cultivating personal relationships with students is the foundation to keeping them engaged in the interACTIVE classroom. From this point, any achievement a student makes will continue to grow and nourish the relationship further. When you're gifted a new class of students, you may struggle to find the time to personally get to know each student. Finding and adopting even one

strategy for doing this is a step in the right direction toward positively impacting students through your individual relationships with them.

TEACHER POSTCARDS—Sharing your thoughts and feelings is one of the easiest ways to build a relationship with your students. Sending short, sweet notes of encouragement home for students to find is one easy way to reach out and build a relationship with them. During an open house or Meet the Teacher event, leave a pile of blank postcards on a table and ask students (parents can help!) to take a card and address it to themselves. Leave a small basket or bin where students can leave their addressed card and then store them somewhere safe. Throughout the year, as students accomplish something they are proud of or achieve a new goal, pull out their postcard and write them a quick note of encouragement. Smack a stamp on it and mail it. You have now acknowledged your student's accomplishment and sent it home to be celebrated. Students will come running into class excited to relive the moment they received your note. And don't be surprised if a parent or two emails you a quick note sharing their surprise and delight over your extra effort. This simple act may take a few extra minutes, but you will create a memorable connection, and it will continue to grow for the rest of the year.

BIRTHDAY BOOKS—Students' birthdays are the one day when they get to celebrate *them*! Whether your school strictly outlaws sweets or fully embraces celebrating, giving students a small gift on their birthday is a great way to build a relationship with them. It's as easy as keeping a small bin of various "birthday books" for students to choose from on their special day. These books should be age appropriate and leveled depending on the grade you teach, and the more variety you can include, the better. You can either recommend a book for students based on your relationship with them or allow them to choose one personally. Scholastic is a great place to grab books for your box. Every month they offer many books for $1.00, and they are generous about "gifting" teachers with bonus books and points with each order they place.

 Tip: At the beginning of every year, Scholastic runs a *huge* incentive for teachers. If you place an average-sized order through your class, you can receive enough bonus points to fund your birthday box for the entire year!

> *"In an effort to help students develop a love of reading, I have implemented the popular idea of Birthday Books in my classroom. This idea is a special way to celebrate each student on their birthday and provide them with choice in selecting a forever book. Not only is it promoting literacy, but students are thrilled to receive a new book from their teacher that they can keep forever."*
>
> —Brandi Miller (@bmilla84)

ACKNOWLEDGING PERSONAL ACCOMPLISHMENTS—As you get to know your students you will be amazed at the various activities they pile on their plates each week—dance, judo, sports such as football, basketball, or soccer, music lessons, and volunteering. You name it, and there's a chance one of your students participates in it. Another way to build relationships with your students is to support them by attending one of their activities. It is grandiose to think you will be able to see all of them take part in one of their hobbies, but perhaps you could see half of them. Consider asking students and parents at your Meet the Teacher event to send you their upcoming schedule of games and practices. Or send a reminder once a month in your newsletter. In our classrooms, we set a routine with students to give us at least two weeks' notice if they would like us to visit. Our students know we have busy lives with our own two young children, and we have to plan ahead to make time in our schedule. We often take our children with us and have found they enjoy getting to see other students from school in a new setting. This helps build an even stronger sense of family among students from all grades at school. And don't feel you need to stay for the entire event. An inning, one dance routine, or part of one half of a game is all it takes for you to show you care, growing the relationship between you and your students.

 Tip: If you have a social media account, ask your students to tag you in photos of them dancing, scoring goals, and doing what they find exciting. This allows you to "be in more places at once" and also gives students the ability to choose what they want to share with you.

BE POSITIVE

You can accomplish so much simply by having a positive outlook on life. As a teacher, it is your job to be the encouragement for your students when they can't seem to find it themselves. Being positive can benefit your classroom in numerous ways, and building relationships with students is one of them.

TEAM BUILDING—"Teamwork makes the dream work" may be an overused saying, but there is much truth to it. Students need to feel safe and wanted in their classroom—not just with the teacher but also with their peers. In classrooms filled with diversity, it is crucial to introduce students to each other in the first few weeks and help them see each other's strengths and uniqueness. We try to build a lot of team building activities into our lessons throughout the year, but during the first two weeks of school, we integrate one into our learning almost daily. Below we have listed some of our favorites for you to try with your students!

 Tip: Don't forget! Always start planning a lesson with your standard or learning goal in mind, and then build out from there. Included below are both the activities and the subject area we try to embed team building into.

Activity	Description
My Mouth Is a Volcano **by Julia Cook** 	Read this book at the beginning of the year when talking about the power of words. After you read, ask the kids to work in pairs or groups to create their own mini volcanoes with the easy vinegar and baking soda reaction—and shoot them off!
Two Truths and a Lie	Use this activity within the first week of school to help students get to know each other and find similarities between themselves. Realizing they have something in common with one another helps students build relationships. In this activity, students come up with three facts about themselves: two are true and one is not. They share these with the class, and everyone discusses and votes on the one they think is the "lie." You can do this in a whole group circle on the carpet, in small table groups, or even digitally using Flipgrid.

Class Cranium Read Aloud 	This activity allows students to work through content in a similar fashion to a popular board game. Complete the read aloud and discuss the importance of following the rules in class. Then create a list of class rules together and ask the students to work in groups to guess the rules Cranium style: students roll a die and have to either draw, sculpt, or act out a clue to help their team guess the rule. Use this die template, and all you need is a pencil for drawing and a small tub of Play-doh! *What if Everybody Did That?* by Ellen Javernick and Colleen M. Madden
Weight of Words 	Penny boats are a classic activity to use at the beginning of the year, but why not pair them with a lesson on the weight of one's words! You could use many different books to introduce this activity. Then give students several sheets of tin foil and an allotted amount of time to build a boat. The goal is to build a boat that can hold the most weight in pennies. After the STEM (science, technology, engineering, and math) activity, discuss how negative words weigh us down by adding pennies to the boat while students watch it sink lower and lower into the water. *The Invisible Boy* by Trudy Ludwig *Stick and Stone* by Beth Ferry and Tom Lichtenheld *One* by Kathryn Otoshi
STEM lesson 	If your school has a theme each year like ours does, this lesson is a great way to integrate the theme with team building. Start with the read-aloud and discuss the hardships of trying to complete a task amid failure. You can easily integrate programs like Leader in Me or concepts such as GRIT if your school uses them. After reading, have a team building contest correlating with your theme. For example, when our school's theme was "Legendary Learners," we asked the students to build a catapult for marbles. *The Most Magnificent Thing* by Ashley Spires Want more information on GRIT? Want more information on Leader in Me?

Art Integration	This activity is a spin-off of the Kindness Rocks Project. Start by reading *Only One You* with its amazing illustrations using mixed media of real painted rocks. The story focuses on becoming responsible for your own decisions, and it follows a father as he guides his son through all the things he needs to know before swimming into the big world. After reading, you could allow students to paint their own rock representing who they are, and then share with the class.
	*Only One You* by Linda Kranz 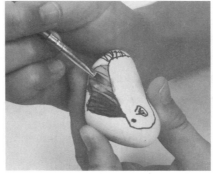 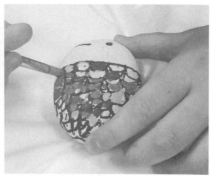
Believe in Your #selfie	This is a simple and easy way for kids to get to know each other at the beginning of the year. Students use cutout hashtags and come up with a word to describe themselves. You can layer this project as much or as little as you want. Simply ask the students to write or decorate their word, or you can add video using Flipgrid, giving the students a chance to explain their word and why they chose it. Take a photo of each child. Adhere each student's word to his or her photo, laminate, and hang on a bulletin board or door display. Voila! You have an amazing way to represent each student.

RECOGNITIONS AND AWARDS—Awarding children for a positive action or behavior has been proven to be far more productive than disciplining them for a negative one. Don't wait for the school to give awards; use your positive relationships with your students to recognize the great things they are doing. You can award students' accomplishments in several quick, easy, and personal ways:

POSITIVE REFERRALS—Rewarding students for positive behavior is easy through the use of positive referrals. This simple act of sending a favorable note home can have a huge impact on students and families alike. You can also let students nominate each other for positive "awards" throughout the day.

CALL HOME—When you don't have a lot of extra time to send home positive referrals, try a call home! It takes only a few minutes and is another easy way to share with parents the positive things their student is doing in the classroom. Carve out a few extra minutes and let the student make the call with you! If no one picks up, no worries! Leave a positive message for parents to stumble on later in the day.

"MOVING UP" AWARDS—It's easy to get caught up in the excitement at the end of the year (there are awards and kids are looking forward to moving on)—but moving on is hard for some. Giving special awards is a way to make this season more positive for all students by creating some fun end-of-year awards where you hold a ceremony to recognize each student for his or her unique character traits and learner qualities.

MUSICAL SONG INTRODUCTIONS—For a fun and positive beginning of the year icebreaker, ask your students to choose one song to describe them (and do so without telling anyone else what they pick!). Each day play one of the songs. We like to do this during pack-up before dismissal, but you also could do it in the morning when students arrive, during a brain break, or use it as a daily transition song, where it is played repeatedly. Without telling anyone who the song belongs to, let it play and watch the students try to figure out who chose it, sparking conversations with each other and with you. When the song is finished playing, gather students in one spot and ask the student who chose the song to stand up, explain why she chose it, and share a bit about herself. This is an easy and non-intimidating way for students to share a bit about themselves—and provides the additional positive bonus of often making students want to sing, dance, and smile!

 Be Warned: Students will enjoy this so much, they will ask repeatedly to choose songs to share with each other. What was meant to be used as an icebreaker can easily become a quarterly tradition!

BE PROACTIVE

While being positive and putting your own personal touch on things is important, often you also need to be proactive and seek out positive interactions with your students. For some students, this is the only way you will be able to build and develop a relationship with them. Coming up with ways to interact with those quiet and withdrawn students may be difficult, but it will yield rich rewards in the end—not just with those shyer students, but with all of them!

NAME MEMORIZATION—Nothing makes new and nervous students feel comfortable like their new teacher greeting them warmly with their name. Their faces instantly light up, their jaws drop, and *you* have instantly made a positive connection for the rest of the year—showing your students you value them and that they have a special place in your classroom. But learning the names of new students by the time school starts can be challenging. If your school is like ours, you only receive your list of names a couple of days before your Meet the Teacher event. This makes it tough to be prepared for your students' arrival—especially amid the normal chaos of getting ready for school to start. You might benefit from a "trick" we do to learn our new students' names. At the end of each school year, we buy a yearbook. When we receive our new list of students in August, we use our yearbook as a reference! We look up the students, and if their photo can be found, we create flashcards to use prior to meeting them. Whether the flashcards are made using a copy machine or created digitally is irrelevant; our concern is matching names with faces. When the day arrives to meet and greet our new students, we're better prepared, and the fun begins.

STUDENT SURVEY FORMS—Being proactive inherently implies you are seeking information students are not freely giving. Students have an opinion about nearly everything, even if they don't tell you. And sometimes you forget to ask. (Or, honestly, if you're like us, you forget *often*. A *lot* of the time. Almost *always*.) A great way to stay connected with your students while also building a relationship with them is by using a simple survey. You can do this through any platform (e.g., Microsoft or Google), or you can conduct an "old-fashioned" survey using paper and pencil. The idea is simply to give students a chance to share their feelings and thoughts on various aspects of their class. You can give them a simple survey each morning to find out how they are feeling before starting their learning for the day. Or give them a chance to review a recent project they had to complete or a new program or app they used in class. A short, simple form allows students to voice their opinion or share their feelings on things beyond academics. It gives them a chance to be heard. And if you give a survey or a form, you *must* listen! Simply giving students the form doesn't automatically make them

Here is a simple example of a mood survey we keep up in our classroom.

feel included or strengthen your relationship. It is when you listen and make changes that students see you value their voice and opinion.

GOOD MORNING GREETINGS—Nothing starts off a day better than a warm greet-

---

SIMPLY GIVING STUDENTS THE FORM DOESN'T AUTOMATICALLY MAKE THEM FEEL INCLUDED OR STRENGTHEN YOUR RELATIONSHIP. IT IS WHEN YOU LISTEN AND MAKE CHANGES THAT STUDENTS SEE YOU VALUE THEIR VOICE AND OPINION.

---

ing. Whether you pick up your students from a holding area or meet them at the door, the simple gesture of greeting each one individually is an easy—yet proactive—way to build relationships with your students. And don't just say "good morning" or deliver a blanket greeting; rather, acknowledge each student individually *by name*. You will set the tone for the day, boost their overall engagement, and contribute to their individual sense of belonging in the class. Some teachers take this greeting to the next level, creating and memorizing handshakes for every student. Regardless of how you greet students, make a point to acknowledge them every morning before the day begins.

PERSONAL HANDSHAKES AND HUMOR—You don't *have* to create unique handshakes with all of your students to make them feel special. Sometimes a class handshake is the best option. During the first few weeks of school, teach the students one handshake (check out some great video examples on GoNoodle by Koo Koo Kanga Roo). Then anytime something exciting or positive happens, your students can give each other the "Jazzy Jeff" handshake and walk away with a sense of pride. Laughter and humor help comfort your students while creating a positive learning environment. Always try to embarrass yourself during the first few weeks of school. This shows your students you make mistakes, too, and you can laugh at yourself. Once you've captured this level of comfort, your students won't be shy or afraid to share their thinking—a good thing, since they will learn more from incorrect responses than correct ones.

INCLUDING PARENTS IN THE INTERACTIVE CLASS

CHAPTER 6

INCLUDE *VERB*

\ in-ˈklüd \

BEING PART OF A WHOLE

Parents look at their students' classroom and how it functions slightly differently than teachers do. Because of this, it is important for teachers to consider their point of view when interacting with them. Teachers need to put on "parent glasses" and try to digest *our* world from *their* perspective.

OPENING THE WINDOW TO THE CLASSROOM

To better understand a parent's perspective of education, think of someone who wears glasses—maybe even yourself! Your glasses help you see, or maybe you're completely dependent on them to function effectively. What happens when you take off your glasses? You view the world entirely differently. You have a sense of where things are located but you can't see clearly. Everything is blurred. You might be able to tell where people are located in a room by their movement or the sound of their voices, but you can't recognize them.

This is how parents often view your classroom. They know the basics of the school—when to drop off or pick up, how to register to volunteer or chaperone a field trip, the way grading is done, and when report cards come out. Depending on how you communicate with them, they may even know what standards and content you will cover in class during the week. Even so, most parents feel out of place and uncomfortable at school and around the classroom. They haven't been students in a long time, and they may be unfamiliar with the acronyms and red tape of the current educational system. They want to help their children, but they don't know how and often just try to stay out of the way. As a result, they have limited knowledge of what you are teaching and how their children are learning, despite your most valiant efforts to communicate with them.

Over the past few years, we have developed a solution for this. We call it "opening the window to the classroom." When our firstborn started kindergarten, we started to shift our teaching. For the first time, we realized what our classroom parents experienced. After we sent our son to school for an entire day, we anxiously awaited the bell at dismissal, excited to talk to him about all the learning he did. But each afternoon, he returned with an anticlimactic "fine" or "good." He loved the kids in his class, his teacher was nice, and his daily routine was pleasant, but we weren't able to experience any of this with him. We longed to talk to him about what he had learned and share in the joy he clearly felt while at school, but his ability to remember parts to share with us was—well…we'll just say it "needed improvement."

We realized we were not the only parents who felt this way; many others also wished to support and encourage their children's learning. Teachers have an army of parents willing to work with their children at home to enrich and extend what is taught at school. But the army needs communication from you. How are you opening your classroom window to let parents see inside?

In what ways do you communicate with parents so they can support you at home? We've shared below some of our favorite ways to get parents interAC-TIVE and involved!

GETTING PARENTS INVOLVED

PARENT MAGNETS

One great way to open the window of communication from the beginning of the year is to use "teacher magnets" containing your contact information. Parents can hang these on the fridge and keep your contact information handy all year long! They'll no longer need to send handwritten notes to you or trek to the school website for your email address.

Magnets are also handy because they're *not* paper. Think about it. Teachers often meet parents for the first time at a Meet the Teacher event. Parents come—along with *all* the other parents, grandparents, and siblings of *all* the other students—with their hands full of supplies and heads full of questions, only to face piles of forms and flyers from the school to take home and fill out, plus additional materials the teacher may give them. Talk about information overload! The teacher magnet can be clipped to the papers to keep your contact information from being buried in the paper pile and make it easily accessible for the parents.

Another positive thing about using the magnets is you're communicating to parents you *want* to talk to them. Think about another aspect of Meet the Teacher. You may be bouncing around the room, trying your best to carry out introductions, find time to speak with both parents and students alike, and simultaneously answer all their questions. While this whirlwind is exciting and exhausting, it's not ideal for communicating to your parents that you *want* to be in contact with them. In fact, sometimes communication at Meet the Teacher resembles only a parent signup list. Using a magnet can communicate a more positive message. These magnets can be as simple or elaborate as you like. We use Vistaprint to make ours, and if you plan in advance you can get coupon codes or find online discounts to make printing reasonable.

Tip: Include on the magnet just your contact information (name, social media handles, email, and phone), but not information likely to change from year to year (room number, grade level, etc.). This way you can order magnets in a larger quantity to get a better price and avoid reordering each year.

You can design and create a file in any software, using the dimensions stated by the printing company. Traditionally, we have made our magnets the size of traditional business cards (3.5 inches by 2 inches). Include your name, email, school phone, and social media accounts, and don't forget to have fun with your design! Incorporate your school colors or yearly theme. Throw in a fun Bitmoji image, Emoji, or clip art. Create an inviting image, designed to welcome families to contact you.

WEEKLY PARENT COMMUNICATION

Another effective way to keep parents in touch with your classroom happenings is to send a weekly "preview" email. We suggest sending these emails *before* the upcoming week, so the information is current and relevant. Too often teachers send information to parents *after* the week is over. You don't want parents to feel your communication with them is an afterthought.

You can format weekly communication in many ways, and none is right or better than another. We view communication as an integral part of an interACTIVE classroom and have found ourselves using several different forms in our growth as interACTIVE teachers. Where do you fall?

HARDCOPY FLYER—This is the most traditional form of communication teachers use with parents. They type and format the newsletter, print it, and send it home with students—crossing their fingers and hoping it makes its way into the hands of the parents. If you choose this type of communication, we challenge you to make it more interACTIVE by adding QR codes to showcase student work, take parents to various websites, or involve them in interACTIVE lessons.

EMAIL UPDATES—Email eliminates the need for a student "go-between" and ensures your communication reaches the parents. A weekly email update is basically the same as the hardcopy flier, but you can send information more rapidly. The internet allows us 24/7 access to other people with the simple click of a button. When you send emails, do your best to keep your sentences short and your communication concise. If it gets too lengthy, parents may skim it or trash it!

MAIL LIST—Currently, this is our favorite form of weekly parent communication. By using a mail server such as MailChimp, you can organize and format your emails more easily than ever! You can insert images, photographs, and videos with a few simple clicks—and without the struggle of extensive web design. Information is now streamlined in a clean, clear way. It is visually appealing and easily condensed into small, digestible bites for busy parents. Another benefit of using mail servers is they generally allow you to schedule when to send your emails. Construct and complete your thoughts throughout the week, schedule a time for the email to go to all your parents, and then forget about it! This feature takes some responsibility off the plates of busy teachers.

UPDATE VIDEOS—The fastest way to share information with someone is to tell them face to face! Have you ever thought of creating a truly interACTIVE newsletter by communicating with parents by video? Take one to two minutes to run through content you will be covering, remind about any coming assessments, and alert parents and students about fun and interACTIVE lessons coming in the next week. The complexity and the formatting of the videos are entirely up to you. You can go basic and record yourself in the corner of your classroom, or use simple video editing apps like iMovie, Adobe Spark Video, or Apple Clips to allow for some basic editing and embellishments such as music and stickers.

DAILY OR WEEKLY RECAP VIDEOS

The power of video summarizes the new generation of learners. Video is not merely a trend, but the primary way millions of people consume content. Videos allow them to take in information at a much higher rate while simultaneously evoking emotions. In addition to using video for weekly updates, try using it to recap the week's events. Start with a simple goal of taking two photos a day—perhaps the covers of books you read, work scribbled on the board, students working collaboratively together in small groups, or completed projects. If it happens in the classroom, document it! When Friday is finished, take the photos, drop them into one of the many photo editing apps, and create a quick "Week in Review" video. You can share the video by embedding it into an email, dropping it into individual student portfolios, or through social media. Now parents have a "fly on the wall" view of your classroom and all the learning going on!

Several different programs allow you to create easy and quality videos for the classroom:

App	Platform	Price	Description
iMovie	iOS and Mac	Free (on newer Apple devices)	Create videos and Hollywood-style trailers. Quickly share a clip (or a portion of a clip), trim, mute, or speed up your videos.
Apple Clips	iOS only	Free	Clips lets you create videos in real time with simple controls: no timeline, tracks, or complicated editing tools. Record video, take photos, or add them from your library. Easily mute audio, adjust the length of your clips, and reorder them. Additionally, Clips allows you to create animated titles and captions using just your voice.
Magisto	iOS, Android, Website	Free and paid options	Great video editor for people on the move and for those who don't have formal video editing skills. Create videos in minutes and share instantly!
MoShow	iOS, Android	Free and paid options	Quickly turn your photos into a fun, attention-grabbing slideshow video. Use a single photo or a collection of pictures and transform static shots.

ONLINE PORTFOLIOS

Individual student portfolios are another excellent way to create interACTIVE experiences for parents. Many programs are available to teachers, ranging from the classroom level to school- or district-wide integration. Regardless of the platform you choose, an online portfolio allows teachers to share with parents the multitude of objects and experiences never making it home—the scribbles on the whiteboard, the plays performed in front of an audience, and the accomplishments made during a small group lesson. These can easily be documented with a photo or video, uploaded, and sent out. In addition to having access to test scores and physical handouts, parents can now also see the many smaller—but just as significant—learning moments. Online portfolios are also a powerful way to share the classic school project, whether it be a book report, group presentation, or STEM project. Teachers often send these projects home to be completed, but how often do parents get to see the final results? With an online portfolio, all the teacher needs to do is take a short video of the presentation and tap a few simple clicks, and the parents can share immediately in their children's accomplishments—instead of waiting for one or two scheduled times during the year to see their progress.

Listed below are some of our favorite ways to create digital portfolios, offering easy ways to get started:

App	Description	Tip
Flipgrid	Social video platform in which educators spark discussions by posting topics to a classroom, school, professional learning community, or public Grid. Students record, upload, view, react, and respond to each other through short videos.	Create a Grid for each student where they can share highlights. After they have built their portfolio, create a MixTape to share with parents, or enable "Guest Mode" to provide parental access.
SeeSaw	Student-driven digital portfolio to inspire your students to do their best work and save you time. Quickly share with class parents what happened throughout the day in just three clicks!	Be sure to include artifacts from the beginning and end of the year to show student progress. Parents will love seeing this!
Buncee	Creation and presentation tool that makes it easy for you and your students to create content for all classroom purposes. Easily share direct links with parents!	Ask each student to create a Buncee where they can add their "best work" throughout the year. Share this with parents!

PARENT HOMEWORK ASSIGNMENTS

We do not assign nightly homework to our students. (While we could discuss our decision at length, we simply recommend you read *Ditch That Homework* by Matt Miller and Alice Keeler.) We do, however, assign homework to *par-*

ents, incorporating it as a way to engage and interact with them. Once a week or once a month, after we have fully covered a specific skill in reading, math, or science (or any subject really!), we send home a specific challenge for family members—a challenge to be taught by their student. Asking students to "re-teach" a skill to their family members is a simple and fun way to engage them with classroom content while allowing parents to be part of the lessons. Our favorite way to do this is by using Flipgrid. The student and family members record a quick video while they complete the task or show their results afterward, and later the students report back to the class.

SOCIAL MEDIA ACCOUNTS

Social media completely changed every aspect of our teaching—including our parent relationships. Social media has been one of the best ways we have connected and interacted with the families of our students. We definitely recommend, when learning something new, be the "technology turtle"—slow and steady. Don't try too many things at once. It often leads to feeling overwhelmed and gaining a subpar level of mastery. The first year we started using social media, we shared on only one platform: Twitter. Each year afterward, we branched out and learned a new platform, depending on our own comfort level and input we received from parents. Today we share information with parents on Instagram, Facebook, and Twitter.

Looking for a way to connect?
Use these handouts to get started!

Today when we mention using social media with students, we instantly encounter conversations regarding privacy. While there is certainly a fear surrounding social media in schools, in our twenty-plus years of combined teaching, we have never had a parent refuse or decline their child's participation. In fact, family members use various forms of social media just as much as, if not more than, our students, and they appreciate the information landing right on their screen in front of them. No searching for a website or memorizing a login code. Family members receive information on their child's classroom in the same feed they already visit daily.

 Disclaimer: Make sure you understand and follow your school's or district's social media policy. Our school has a form we use district-wide giving permission for students to be photographed or filmed on websites and social media, including news outlets and in the yearbook.

BECOMING AN INTERACTIVE EDUCATOR

CHAPTER 7

CONNECT *VERB*

\ kə-ˈnekt \

TO ESTABLISH COMMUNICATION BETWEEN; PUT IN COMMUNICATION

@TheMerrillsEDU

People—including your students and you—are influenced by those they surround themselves with. Who do *you* surround yourself with? This may appear to be a simple and even irrelevant question, but as you reflect on it, you may discover your answer is not what you'd assume. If you're like the majority of teachers we know, you arrive at school hours before your class arrives to prepare lessons, spend your day teaching and engaging students, race through a shorter-than-desired lunch, teach again right up until dismissal time, stay into the evening to prepare fully for the following day, walk to your car (one of the last in the parking lot), drive home to spend more time grading, reading, and preparing, and finally fall into bed—exhausted. (If this schedule doesn't resemble *your* typical day, consider yourself blessed!)

If you want to become an interACTIVE teacher, you need to surround yourself with other interACTIVE teachers. But with a schedule like the one just described, you likely have little time to seek out new learning or connect with fellow educators. Fortunately, there are several easy things you can do to influence the teaching and learning taking place in your classroom while simultaneously growing and improving your craft.

TOOLS FOR CONNECTING AND GROWING

JOIN TWITTER

Ours is not the first book to explain the benefits the small "blue bird" can have on your teaching and learning, and ours will not be the last. If you do not have a Twitter account, stop right now and make one. Seriously. Don't continue reading until you have given yourself the free access to one of the best personal learning networks (PLN) available.

Twitter is a fast-paced, 24/7 hub of communication. We will briefly discuss the power of blogging and sharing ideas through personal posting, but for now think of Twitter as microblogging. Through Twitter, people communicate with a limited number of characters, summarizing their ideas into a single, essential one. It's a place where you can read small, digestible, clear-cut, and concise chunks of information. Twitter is the perfect place for tired, time-crunched teachers!

Millions of people besides teachers use Twitter, but are you aware that of the half a billion tweets posted every day, 4.2 million are related to education? For a teacher who is tired and strapped for time, this platform is a place to beg, borrow, steal (and share!) ideas. The best part? It can all be done in a few clicks!

You can interact with Twitter in many ways, and as you become more familiar with it, you will find yourself fluidly moving through the continuum. For now, here are some tips to help you get started:

LURK—Start by simply joining and following a core set of educators. (We have included below some of our favorites to get you started.) Be broad and choose a differentiated set of people to follow to give you a variety of tweets as you scroll through your feed each time. Read what they share to gain ideas, inspiration, and confirmation about your current practices.

COMMENT—Once you are comfortable with the platform, start interacting by leaving "likes" or comments on posts you connect with. This will lead to people following you, and you will be on your journey of learning from and sharing with others. These connections can turn into friendship and even partnerships. Some of our closest friends today are fellow educators we first met through Twitter.

SHARE—When you have one of those conversations, lessons, or learning moments that completely solidify why you teach and keep you going into the next day, take a photo or video and share it with your fellow Tweetchers. It doesn't have to be long—you only have 280 characters, but the things you find encouraging and motivation will encourage and motivate others. Share your ideas with others!

PARTICIPATE—Twitter is interactive and the best place to participate with other educators online. Every night, various "chats" or ongoing conversations are held between educators, all set up in simple question-and-answer formats and spanning all sorts of topics. The majority are held in the evening and range from fifteen to fifty minutes. Now the time-crunched teachers can sit in their pajamas from the comfort of their homes and connecting with fellow goal-oriented and like-minded educators.

Ready to Get Connected?

Looking to dive into Twitter? Here is a list of some of our favorite educators, speakers, and authors we recommend following:

"I would encourage anyone new to edtech to join Twitter. Twitter is a great starting point for educators to get their feet wet at their own pace. They will be able to explore areas of passion, find people with similar interests, and begin curating their PLN. This will help connect them to information and individuals who can support and guide them as they gain confidence to try new tools or approaches."

—Kathrina Mendez, @kathrina_mendez

INSTRUCTIONAL ROUNDS

You may not realize it, but you are sitting on a treasure trove of learning! Every school is full of experts—experts in classroom management, curriculum, relationships, flexible seating, and so much more! You may know your colleagues' names and room numbers, but when was the last time you visited one of their classrooms? Reach out and take advantage of the experience within your school building. And who better to ask for help than your administration? They pass in and out of all the classrooms and are a great resource to help you identify who might be able to help you. Sitting in another colleague's room for a few minutes can be a refreshing way to reflect and grow as an educator. You will leave with new ideas to try in your own room, or your own routines, procedures, and expectations will be validated. This experience helps you discard bad teaching habits and embrace better ones. It also enables you to reflect on your own teaching practices while getting ideas from others. In the words of Confucius, "Learning without reflection is a waste. Reflection without learning is dangerous."

> **Want to give it a try?**
> One way to get into other classrooms is to first invite colleagues into yours. "Observe Me" signs are an easy way to let others know you welcome feedback and are looking to both learn and share best practices with others.

SKYPE

If venturing into another classroom isn't within your comfort zone, break down your classroom walls while staying inside them. If you have a computer, laptop, or Chromebook in your classroom, you can enter a classroom of another teacher anywhere in the world. Google Hangouts, Skype, Zoom, and Microsoft Teams all function similarly. Start small with a simple activity such as "Guess My Location," where two classrooms take turns sharing camera time asking each other questions. The goal is for students to guess where the other class is located. You could foster this relationship by adding a read-aloud or partnering up students for a continuing penpal assignment. Whether you make this a fun, one-time experience or one lasting all year, a simple webcam is all you need to break down the walls of your class!

> **Want to give it a try?**
> Skype can be used in various ways in the classroom, and a great place to start your journey is through Microsoft EDU's platform. Skype can be used for virtual field trips, to connect with other classrooms across the globe, to invite guest speakers into the classroom, and so much more! Here you can explore resources and find ways to get your classroom connected to the world!
>
> Sign up for free!

BLOGGING

Imagine the end of the day has arrived, and you've successfully pulled off another stellar lesson, complete with a room transformation, a costume change, and some sort of engaging activity. Fabulous! But how can you take this lesson and extend it even further? Blog about it! Blogging is an easy way to share with fellow educators both near and far your ideas, lessons, trials, errors—and stellar successes. The term itself comes straight out of the millennial dictionary. A blog (shortened from "weblog") is an online journal or website where one can post ideas, share videos or pictures, and receive comments from readers. Essentially, it is a website with added interaction, updated regularly instead of sitting stagnant with the same information for long periods of time. Blogs are a great way to connect with fellow educators and share ideas. They provide an easy way to extend learning beyond your four walls and get maximum return on your initial investment. Blogging is beneficial for the writer and the reader and can be done on your own time at your own pace.

As the writer, you are able to curate your ideas. You have a place to house all of your past, present, and future lesson ideas, your unexpected learning moments, and tips and tricks for anyone who is interested to enjoy. As a reader you are able to connect with educators who share a similar teaching style to you, or maybe you'll discover a teacher with lessons covering the same content material you are introducing in your classroom. Another benefit is just connecting with and sharing ideas with teachers who understand your situation— because the students they teach are the same age as yours. Regardless of what you connect over, writing about and reading the ideas of others will influence your own interACTIVE teaching.

WANT TO GIVE IT A TRY?

Starting a blog is easy. In just a few steps, you can become interACTIVE and begin sharing your ideas with people from near and far! Start with a name. Come up with something memorable and related to what you will be sharing. Choose an online host, customize your blog using templates, and tweak it until it looks the way you want. Finally, publish your first post and start promoting your site to other educators in your learning network! On the following page are some great options to choose from when looking to start a blog.

	Pros	Cons
Word Press	• Free • User has complete control • User can move blog to any website • Huge collection of extensions, add-ons, and plug-ins • Easy to customize, thousands of website designs and templates	• You are responsible for security, making backups, and installing updates • No drag and drop (though there's a plug-in for that!) • Does require some basic HTML and CSS knowledge
Blogger	• Free • Easily set up a custom domain (yourname.com) • If you have a Google account, you already have a Blogger account • Simple to set up and use; similar to a Word document	• Customer support • HTML and CSS is editable, but can be overwhelming for newbies • No third-party apps or integrations
Tumblr	• Free (premium versions ranging from $9-$49) • Simplicity (you can get started in a minimal amount of time) • Strong community makes it easy to grow an audience • Schedule posts • Analytics • Mobile optimized	• Design limitations • Functionality limitations • More images and less text perform best • Server-dependent (you must use Tumblr's servers to host your blog)
Weebly	• Free (premium options available) • No caps on pages or storage space • No ads with the first paid tier • Drag and drop elements available • Easy signup • Allows third-party apps	• May be difficult if you are planning to start a blog with lots of pages • Difficult to transfer your blog without copying and pasting it all (if you ever decide to go to another host)
Wix	• Free (premium options available) • Create your blog quickly • Lots of design templates to choose from • Drag and drop from anywhere (but this could quickly turn into a con if you're not careful) • AI (artificial intelligence) design handles a lot of manual work so you don't have to	• Starter plans do not remove ads from your site • Editing and page layout process • Limited features • Limited apps and extensions (most don't add functionality to your blog; they just add an iFrame) • Sites use Flash (which may not be fully functional for mobile viewers)

PODCASTS

When you are strapped for time, podcasts are a great alternative to blogs. Rather than written words, podcasts are digital audio files you can download to a phone or computer, making them available to listen to at your convenience. Podcasts are generally produced in a series, and you can sign up to receive new installments as they are released. You can listen to podcasts almost anywhere you listen to music—during a workout, while folding laundry, on a morning commute, while cooking dinner, on a quick trip to the grocery store, or before bed. The choice is yours. Podcasts are an excellent way to use time and make even mundane daily tasks more productive. With smart speakers like Alexa, Apple Pod, and Google Home, the places and ways you can listen are limitless. If you like the idea and philosophy behind blogging, but don't think you can find the time to sit down long enough to write and edit your ideas, creating your own podcast may be a good fit for you.

WANT TO GIVE IT A TRY?

LISTEN—Podcasts have been around for a while but have become well-known and popular in the last few years. If you want a place to start, here are a few we enjoy tuning in to. Remember to start small and listen to a few episodes of each before subscribing.

- *Ditch That Textbook* by Matt Miller
- *The Infused Classroom* by Holly Clark and Tanya Avrith
- *Cult of Pedagogy* by Jennifer Gonzalez
- *The Google Teacher Tribe* by Matt Miller and Kasey Bell
- *Educational Duct Tape* by Jake Miller
- *Shukes and Giff* by Kim Pollishuke and Jen Giffen
- *House of EdTech* by Chris Nesi
- *TED Radio Hour* hosted by Host Guy Raz
- *Leader of Learning* by Dan Kreiness

CREATE—If you are interested in starting your own podcast, there are many inexpensive apps you can use at home. Podcasts are a great way to share information with fellow colleagues or create episodes for your students to listen to. You can even allow them to create a podcast! Below are some resources and tools we found helpful for creating a podcast.

- Anchor App: Free!

- Alitu: The Podcast Maker $$
- Podbean Podcast App $
- Spreaker Studio $

Royalty-Free Background Music:

"For me, the key to integrating Ed Tech in the classroom successfully, is to know your purpose. When you know what you want as a product at the end of a lesson, it's easier to search and/or ask for help on social media. It's also key to know you are not alone. Even if you are the only one at your grade level who is using a certain app or site, or wanting to explore and do more, you are not alone. People who are passionate about Ed Tech have been in your shoes. Your questions aren't "dumb questions" when you ask. They are well-received and happily answered. Get on Twitter and start asking questions to find your tribe."

—@MrsHeikes

ENGAGING
APPS AND LESSONS

FLIPGRID

WHAT IS IT?

Flipgrid is the leading video discussion platform in which students record short, authentic videos in response to a teacher-created topic. You can create a grid community for your classroom, school, PLC, families, and much more! As the educator, you are the Topic designer with specialized resources and attachments. You can easily create countless conversations between your students and you in just a few effortless clicks.

WHERE CAN I USE IT?

Flipgrid is a web-based program so it can be accessed on iOS, Android, and Windows 10 apps.

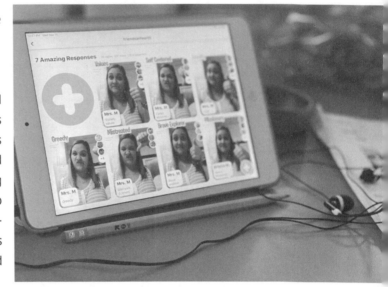

HOW DOES IT WORK?

Think of Flipgrid as a digital bulletin board, filled throughout the year with various *Topics*. Students *reply* to Topics and can also *respond* to replies when given access by the teacher to do so. Flipgrid gives 100 percent control to teachers by allowing them to turn numerous features—such as video response time, video moderation, and selfie decorations—on and off as needed. Flipgrid also gives teachers many options for sharing videos created with family and community outside of the Grid.

HOW CAN I USE IT IN THE CLASSROOM?

Flipgrid is versatile and can be used for any type of activity or event, no matter how big or small. Try using it for back-to-school introductions, book talks, self-reflections, student portfolios, interactive homework, sub plans, digital break outs, and projects showcasing student-created work. The possibilities are endless! Flipgrid is a great way for students to verbalize their learning.

NOT SURE WHERE TO START?

These resources were made by Flipgrid users to help those new to the platform!

 New to using Flipgrid? Check out this amazing and **free** course from Holly Clark to get started step by step.

 Head over to the Innovation Station for great ideas and free resources!

GRID

TOPIC

RESPONSE

REPLY

WANT TO CONNECT?
Twitter: @Flipgrid
Website: flipgrid.com
Instagram: Flipgrid

HIGHLIGHTED FEATURES

SHORTS CAMERA: Teachers can create enriching and compelling video stories for school, work, and life to share using the new and improved Shorts Camera!

FLIPGRIDAR: Teachers are able to generate QR codes for both Topics and Grids, but topic videos are now embedded using Augmented Reality (AR). Scan the QR code with the Flipgrid app, and videos will play through the magic of AR. Note: If they are scanned with Native Camera or any QR code reader, they will play the web-based video, not the AR version.

WHITEBOARD/CHALKBOARD: With just the click of a button, the video screen can turn into a virtual whiteboard/chalkboard allowing anyone to show what they know with digital inking. This is great for any type of touch screen device, but it also can be used with a trackpad or mouse.

STICKER IMAGES: Not only can students add stickers to their videos while recording, but now they can add their own photos directly from the camera roll!

TEXT: Students now have the option to insert text onto their videos both before and during recording. They can use this feature to label, explain, or create during the video process.

FILTERS: Color overlays and pixilated Minecraft Mode are great options for getting shy students to participate in a more comfortable way.

STICKY NOTES: When recording, students can create virtual sticky notes on their screen to help them as they record their message. These are only visible to the video creator and are not seen in the final video.

LET THE DICE DECIDE

GRADE LEVEL: 3rd-5th

CONTENT AREA(S): Reading, Science, History

COMFORT LEVEL: Beginner

LESSON FORMAT: Teacher Created

QUICK TIP: Make sure videos are recorded as replies, not responses.

DESCRIPTION

In this lesson, students use Flipgrid to take a set of comprehension questions to the next level.

ISTE STANDARDS

- Educator will use technology to create, adapt, and personalize learning experiences to foster independent learning and accommodate learner differences and needs. (5a)

- Educator will explore and apply instructional design principles to create innovative digital learning environments to engage and support learning. (5c)

LESSON SUMMARY

1. Create a Topic on Flipgrid titled accordingly. Make sure to give any directions and tips in the description.

2. Record a video in the Topic for each question. When taking your selfie for the video, hold up your fingers, make a sign, write on the video, or do something to indicate the number of the question you are posing.

3. Make sure to have dice for each student or group of students corresponding to the number of question videos you created. (If students have up to six questions to answer, they will need one die. Students will need two dice for seven to twelve questions, etc.)

4. Students roll the dice to decide on the question they are going to answer. The number they roll is the question they will respond to.

5. When students click on the video, they will watch the video you created and respond to it in a reply.

6. If a student rolls a number twice, allow them to respond to a classmate's video rather than answering again. Encourage open-ended conversations requiring additional thinking.

Tap to Record
Your video will be awesome!

Question 1

Question 2

Question 4

Question 3

Question 5

Question 6

TEACHER RECORDS EACH QUESTION AS DIFFERENT RESPONSE

CHECK OUT THE EXAMPLE HERE!

STUDENTS RECORD *REPLIES* – NOT RESPONSES

Question 1
59 views 0 likes

Seth M.

Kailey B.

Samantha F.

Question 2
73 views 0 likes

Sophia F.

James M.

Gavin M.

FLIPGRID TV

GRADE LEVEL: Any

CONTENT AREA(S): Any

COMFORT LEVEL: Advanced

LESSON FORMAT: Teacher Created

QUICK TIP: App smash (#AppSmash) with Do Ink Green Screen to make it appear as though you are really inside the television!

DESCRIPTION

In this lesson, the teacher uses Flipgrid to create "channels," or assignments, for the students to flip through, view, and complete.

ISTE STANDARDS

- Educator will model and nurture creativity and creative expression to communicate ideas, knowledge, or connections. (6d)
- Educator will provide alternative ways for students to demonstrate competency and reflect on their learning using technology. (7a)

LESSON SUMMARY

1. Using a green tablecloth (available from your local dollar store), record your tasks in front of a green screen.

2. Search for a Creative Commons, copyright-friendly, or fair use image of a "greenscreen TV" on Google. Pick one you like, and save it to your device's camera roll.

3. Open the Do Ink Green Screen app, tap on the "+" sign on the top layer, and select "image." Find your TV image and upload it. You may need to pinch or zoom to resize it to fit the width of the screen.

4. Tap on the "+" sign on the middle or bottom layer and select "videos." Find your recorded video or task and upload it. You may need to resize it to fit into your green screen TV.

5. Save your new Do Ink video onto your camera roll. Tap the back button to return to the main screen. Then tap the "sharrow" (the share arrow) and select the "export" option. The file will then be saved to the camera roll.

6. Upload the new Do Ink video to Flipgrid Topic and submit.

4 Amazing Responses

73 Replies   1358 views   5.3h Engagement

Tap to Record
Your video will be awesome!

 CHANNEL #4.

CHANNEL #3.

CHANNEL #2.

 CHANNEL #1.

Tip: Post your video(s) as if you are a student. Then you can have as many different questions or tasks as you'd like. When the students go to complete the tasks, explain to them they are **only to respond to you. They should *not* be creating a new response.** This will keep everything organized under the appropriate Topic. See the GIF above for a better understanding! Repeat as necessary!

STUDENTS RECORD
REPLIES - NOT RESPONSES

 CHECK OUT THE EXAMPLE HERE!

PODCAST

GRADE LEVEL: 3rd-5th

CONTENT AREA(S): Any

COMFORT LEVEL: Beginner

LESSON FORMAT: Student Created

QUICK TIP: Have students record their podcast in sections. This way they can more easily edit the audio chunks without having to start over after a small mistake.

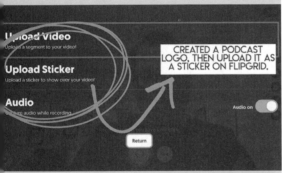

Try app smashing with a creation program such as Adobe Spark Post, which allows students to create their podcast image digitally.

DESCRIPTION
Students can use Flipgrid to create their own podcast station.

ISTE STANDARDS
- Students engage in positive, safe, legal, and ethical behavior when using technology, including social interactions online or when using networked devices. (2b)
- Students communicate complex ideas clearly and effectively by creating or using a variety of digital objects such as visualizations, models, or simulations. (6c)

LESSON SUMMARY
1. Set up the class Grid in Flipgrid before students record. Podcasts may be sorted by Grids or Topics based on your preference. For example, the Grid may be for all of the class's podcasts, and each different podcast gets its own Topic, where students record all their "episodes."
2. Students begin by opening up the shorts camera and choosing either the whiteboard or blackboard option.
3. Students choose the image they want on the screen, using the sticker icon. This could be a drawing or design made by students and uploaded previously to the camera. Once the drawing is chosen, students need to size it accordingly.
4. Underneath the sticker image, using the text tool, students write the text box for their episode title.
5. When they're ready to record, students either press and hold or click the "record" button to begin recording their podcast. Because the white or blackboard feature is enabled, their picture will not appear. Only their voice will record.
6. Students can record their podcast to the length preset for the Grid or Topic by you.
7. When finished, students submit their podcast, which can then be shared out using the multiple "share" features in Flipgrid.

WOULD YOU RATHER?

DESCRIPTION

Students are given a scenario with two choices. They use their number sense to make a choice and use Flipgrid to justify their reasoning.

ISTE STANDARDS

- Educator will use technology to create, adapt, and personalize learning experiences that foster independent learning and accommodate learner differences and needs. (5a)
- Educator will provide alternative ways for students to demonstrate competency and reflect on their learning using technology. (7a)

LESSON SUMMARY

1. Begin by recording a new Topic on Flipgrid. Use the "record video" option to record yourself giving the problem to students.

2. Using the new Shorts camera and whiteboard or blackboard option, students respond to the question, explaining the answer they got and why they reasoned the way they did.

3. Students also may wish to watch the videos recorded by their classmates to compare their thinking with the class's.

GRADE LEVEL: 3rd-5th

CONTENT AREA(S): Math

COMFORT LEVEL: Beginner

LESSON FORMAT: Teacher created

QUICK TIP: These activities work best when you ask questions without a clear or definite answer, allowing more room for discussion.

CHECK OUT A TOPIC IN THE FLIPGRID DISCO LIBRARY ALREADY CREATED FOR THIS LESSON!

SUB PLANS

GRADE LEVEL: 3rd-5th

CONTENT AREA(S): Any

COMFORT LEVEL: Advanced

LESSON FORMAT: Teacher Created

QUICK TIP: Make sure your students are comfortable using Flipgrid before leaving assignments with a substitute. Have a designated class helper in case the substitute needs extra guidance.

DESCRIPTION

The days of writing out pages of sub plans are over! Simply use a Grid to record your assignments using Flipgrid. Create video explanations along with attaching assignments directly within the Grid for seamless workflow while you are away!

ISTE STANDARDS

- Educator will manage the use of technology and student learning strategies in digital platforms, virtual environments, hands-on makerspaces, or in the field. (6b)

- Educator will use technology to create, adapt, and personalize learning experiences to foster independent learning and accommodate learner differences and needs. (5a)

LESSON SUMMARY

1. Create a grid for the day you are away. Suggested titles could include the day of the week, the date, and "sub plans." For example: "Sub Plans for Wednesday, October 26th."

2. Create a Topic for each assignment the kids are to complete. Use the topic video to record directions explaining the assignment.

3. Include up to ten attachments to the Topic that could be used in the assignment. Attachments can be anything with a web link, including Microsoft web files such as PowerPoint or Word, Google Slides or Docs, website links, video links, and much more!

4. Continue adding Topics for each assignment for the day. Leave the Grid information in the plans for the sub.

FLIPGRID SUB PLANS

Notes: Good morning! All of our lessons today are on an online program called Flipgrid. All lessons are located on a grid title with today's date. Each time students are to log in they will use the same code and grid. I may "pop in" occasionally to check in on their work and leave feedback.

TIME	ACTIVITY DESCRIPTION	FLIPCODE & QR ACCESS	MATERIALS NEEDED
8:30–9:00 am	This activity is a morning warm-up/welcome time. Students are to log in and share a goal they have for this week. They may watch peer videos and comment and encourage each other when finished with their own video.	codehere	Students may spread out and move seats in order to find a quiet recording spot.
9:00–10:00 am	For writing, student are going to log in and begin by reading through "A Wonder" article #1024 titled "Are You Strong" pinned to the top of the topic. When finished, students are to use the Word document that is also pinned to the topic to write a paragraph about what makes them strong. They may then record a video summarizing their writing.	codehere	Today students will do all of their writing in the online document, but if they would like, they may use notebook paper for any planning purposes.
10:00–11:00 am	In math today, students will start with a warm up activity titled "Would You Rather?" Student will take time to answer and support their reasoning with evidence. When finished, they may move to the topic titled "Multiplication Magic" and complete the tasks assigned using the resources attached.	codehere	Students may like to have their whiteboards out to work their math out on. They may also use the whiteboard feature within Flipgrid if they choose.
Lunch and Recess			
12:00–1:00	Science will start with kids watching a video on matter. There is a task for students to explore afterwards and a corresponding doc for them to record the findings of their exploration on.	codehere	On the blue counter is a basket with the necessary supplies each group will need sorted accordingly.

 Get Started Now! Download this template to help you get started with creating your first digital sub plan!

PDF Version   Editable PowerPoint Version

 Tip: Try using the Freeze or Moderate feature as a way to slowly push out various topics or different days' assignments.

 This fabulous idea came from the one and only Kyle Hamstra. Connect with him here! Twitter: @kylehamstra

DIGITAL BREAK OUT

GRADE LEVEL: Any

CONTENT AREA(S): Any, Especially Math

COMFORT LEVEL: Medium

LESSON TYPE: Teacher Created

QUICK TIP: Passcodes can be both letters and numbers. Make sure to test the codes as you write your clues. Because many simple words and codes may already be taken, get creative with your answers.

DESCRIPTION

Using the options to password protect both Grids and individual Topics, teachers can create problems that will be "unlocked" when a student enters the correct answer. This will "release" the video assignment or discussion prompt.

ISTE STANDARDS

- Educator will explore and apply instructional design principles to create innovative digital learning environments to engage and support learning. (5c)

- Educator will create learning opportunities to challenge students to use a design process and computational thinking to innovate and solve problems. (6c)

- Educator will model and nurture creativity and creative expression to communicate ideas, knowledge, or connections. (6d)

LESSON SUMMARY

1. Create the puzzles and problems students will work on to "unlock" the lessons before signing in to Flipgrid.

2. First, choose Student ID Grid for the type of grid you will be making. For students to have to break into it, you will need to put your first break out code in as the "flipcode."

3. Instead of placing a list of students in the list, place the second answer code in as the only student ID. This will be how they unlock the topic activity.

4. Now prepare the clues for students ahead of game time and then ready, set, go! Break out!

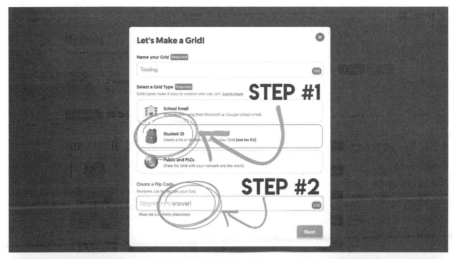

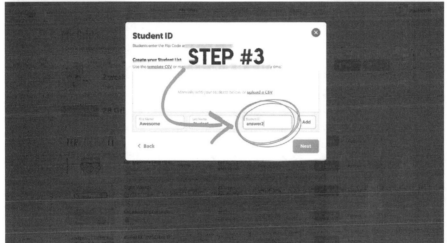

DIGITAL BREAK OUT LESSON IDEAS

- Factors of a number
- Degrees of an angle or angles added together
- Location on a map (name of place, coordinates)
- Names and dates of famous battles, people, events
- Time of day (with a.m. and p.m. included if more characters are needed)
- Place value
- Vocabulary word(s)

CHECK OUT THIS QUICK VIDEO ON HOW TO SET UP A BREAK OUT GRID!

GUESS THE GENRE

GRADE LEVEL: K-2

CONTENT AREA(S): Reading

COMFORT LEVEL: Beginner

LESSON TYPE: Student Created

QUICK TIP: Depending on the length of your reading block, this lesson may work better in two periods because of the illustrating.

DESCRIPTION

Students illustrate their own book cover, using their knowledge of fiction and nonfiction, and then share with the class in the created Flipgrid Topic. Fellow classmates observe the cover and try to guess what genre the created book would fall into by responding to the initial video.

ISTE STANDARDS

- Students create original works or responsibly repurpose or remix digital resources into new creations. (6b)
- Students publish or present content to customize the message and medium for their intended audiences. (6d)

LESSON SUMMARY

1. Introduce the different types of literary genres.

2. Ask students to create a "fake" book cover on a piece of paper.

3. Ask students to introduce their illustration in Flipgrid, where they challenge their peers to see whether they can correctly identify the genre.

4. After a given amount of time, ask the original illustrators to go back and watch the replies to their book cover.

5. Ask the original illustrators to discuss whether the replies are correct or incorrect.

"The use and function of Flipgrid is incredibly simple, which makes it so powerful, from Pre-K through the university level and even beyond connecting communities together."
—Michael Abramczyk (@_on11)

TWO TRUTHS AND A LIE

DESCRIPTION

Use Flipgrid to help students get to know their teacher and new classmates by filming fun "All About Me" videos with a little twist!

ISTE STANDARDS

- Students use digital tools to connect with learners from a variety of backgrounds and cultures, engaging with them in ways to broaden mutual understanding and learning. (7a)

- Students engage in positive, safe, legal, and ethical behavior when using technology, including social interactions online or when using networked devices. (2b)

LESSON SUMMARY

1. Create a Topic entitled "Two Truths and a Lie." You may prefer to set up an entire "Getting to Know You" Grid and use this as one of your Topics for the first week or month.

2. Write out your directions clearly and use the Topic video to record an introduction for your students. In it, include two true statements about yourself and one false statement. Do not hint at which are true.

3. Students log in and record a video the same way you did. They give three statements: two true and one false. They are not to hint at which is the false fact.

4. When finished recording, students may watch the videos created by their classmates and respond to them with their guess at which fact is false.

5. After time is given for all students to respond (this could be one class period, overnight, or after a week), students watch the videos as a group and together try to guess the false fact.

6. Finally, the student stands up and tells the class the true facts and spends time introducing himself or herself to the group.

GRADE LEVEL: Any

CONTENT AREA(S): Back to School or Getting to Know You

COMFORT LEVEL: Beginner

LESSON TYPE: Student Created

QUICK TIP: This is a great activity to send home with students at Meet the Teacher or after the first day of school. Use the QR code feature so the whole family can get involved too!

QR CODE HUNT (FICTION)

GRADE LEVEL: Any

CONTENT AREA(S): Reading

COMFORT LEVEL: Beginner

LESSON TYPE: Teacher Created

QUICK TIP: Try using "book tape" to secure the printed codes in the books to avoid tearing the pages.

DESCRIPTION

Many students struggle with independent reading or small group novel studies. Use this easy, yet interactive approach for monitoring student reading through the use of Flipgrid's QR code feature.

ISTE STANDARDS

- Educator will use technology to create, adapt, and personalize learning experiences to foster independent learning and accommodate learner differences and needs. (5a)

- Educator will foster a culture where students take ownership of their learning goals and outcomes in both independent and group settings. (6a)

- Educator will manage the use of technology and student learning strategies in digital platforms, virtual environments, hands-on makerspaces, or in the field. (6b)

LESSON SUMMARY

1. For this activity, you will start with the questions you want students to answer, the projects you want them to create, or the big ideas you want them to discuss. These can come from worksheets, novel study guides, or just from your own creativity!

2. In Flipgrid, create a grid for the book. Then create a Topic for each activity you want students to complete while reading. Use the Topic video to record yourself giving directions, modeling the activity, or giving an example of an end product. (Hint: Assigning activities by chapter makes it much easier to manage!)

3. When finished, click the "Share" button and click on the QR code image.

Flip Code: 67a013a

Students visit the link below, scan the QR Code, or enter the Flip Code in the Flipgrid app.

https://flipgrid.com/67a013a

Copy

Right-click to copy.

Download

4. Copy the QR code directly from the screen and paste it into a formatting program such as Microsoft Word, Microsoft PowerPoint, or Google Slides. Copy and paste the one QR code as many times as you have students reading the book. You need one QR code per student.

5. Repeat step 4 with the other activities you have for the book. You should end up with one QR code sheet for every activity.

6. Pile up the books and cut and tape all of one QR code into each book. Do this with the rest of the QR codes. When finished, each student reading the book will have secret codes hidden with assignments to complete along the way!

QR CODE HUNT (NONFICTION)

GRADE LEVEL: K-3

CONTENT AREA(S): Reading

COMFORT LEVEL: Beginner

LESSON TYPE: Teacher Created

QUICK TIP: This lesson requires some planning, so it may be best to work collaboratively with a team. Create a new Grid on Flipgrid, then add your team as copilots. Give each person on your team a text feature, and then record your challenges as a student.

DESCRIPTION

Teach your students the importance of text features with this simple, yet engaging activity. Place QR codes next to various text features, and ask the students to scan them as they find them.

ISTE STANDARDS

- Students curate information from digital resources using a variety of tools and methods to create collections of artifacts to demonstrate meaningful connections or conclusions. (3c)
- Students contribute constructively to project teams, assuming various roles and responsibilities to work effectively toward a common goal. (7c)

LESSON SUMMARY

1. Check out several nonfiction books from your media center. You'll want to place your students in groups, and each group will need one or two books.
2. Create a Grid on Flipgrid for the assignment.
3. Find the text features in the books, and create a Topic on Flipgrid for each text feature.
4. In each Topic, record a video representing the appropriate text feature. Upload the videos as a resource on the appropriate grid.
5. Tap on the "Share" icon to generate a QR code.
6. Download and print each QR code (you can use Post-it notes or "book tape" to tape them inside the books).
7. Repeat the printing process for each book or text feature.

 CHECK OUT AN EXAMPLE HERE!

DO INK GREEN SCREEN

WHAT IS IT?

Green Screen by Do Ink makes it easy to create incredible green screen videos and images right on your iPad or iPhone. The app lets you combine photos and videos from the camera roll with live images from your iPad or iPhone camera.

WHERE CAN I USE IT?

Green Screen by Do Ink is only available on iOS devices. It can be purchased at a one-time cost of $2.99. Schools can purchase this app in volume via Apple's VPP program. Schools approved for this program can get the app at a fifty percent discount for orders of twenty or more.

HOW DOES IT WORK?

The green screen effect works by combining images from multiple sources into a single image. The source images are stacked in layers, one in front of the other. Normally, you'd only be able to see the image in front, since it would block your view of the background image. The trick is to make portions of the foreground image transparent, allowing the corresponding parts of the background image to show through. The green screen effect does this by looking for a specific color (like green, for example) in the foreground image and erasing any portions of the image containing this color.

HOW CAN I USE IT IN THE CLASSROOM?

Green Screen by Do Ink can be used as a presentation tool, an extension for writing projects, or as a way for students to try out a STEM job such as a meteorologist. It can also be used as a platform to create classroom morning announcements, and so much more.

TIPS AND TRICKS:

- Have students record videos or take pictures using the camera roll and import the files into Do Ink. This way they don't lose their original files if they make a mistake during editing.

- The quality and color of the backdrop you use makes a difference. Although you can record your video in front of any solid color backdrop, the quality of the results can be improved if your backdrop is a bright, fully saturated color, and if it's made from a matte, nonreflective material.

- Good lighting helps. You don't need special "movie lights," but you'll find your results improve when your backdrop and subject are well lit. Minimizing shadows on your backdrop can also help considerably.

- Consider mounting your iPad on a tripod or stand. Holding your camera still while recording in front of a green screen can improve the quality of your video.

- Experiment with the chroma key color and sensitivity settings. Getting them right makes a big difference.

- Experiment with the distance of your subject from the green screen so as not to have any shadows

- Experiment with the distance of your camera from the subject.

THE TALE OF THE TEACHER GHOST

GRADE LEVEL: Any

CONTENT AREA(S): Math

COMFORT LEVEL: Advanced

LESSON FORMAT: Teacher Created

QUICK TIP: Take a picture of your classroom ahead of time and have a green t-shirt handy. It also helps to have a tripod (or a helper!).

DESCRIPTION

In this lesson, the teacher uses a green screen to create a "ghost" of herself. Then she challenges the class to spooky math problems!

ISTE STANDARDS

- Educator will explore and apply instructional design principles to create innovative digital learning environments to engage and support learning. (5c)

- Educator will create learning opportunities to challenge students to use a design process and computational thinking to innovate and solve problems. (6c)

LESSON SUMMARY

1. Take a photo of your classroom and place it on the bottom layer in the Do Ink Green Screen app by tapping the "+" sign and then "photo" button. Find the picture you want to use and select it.

2. Using the middle layer, tap the "+" sign and then tap "camera."

3. Slip the green t-shirt over your head and place a familiar item over your head (like a pair of glasses or a hat).

4. Press the record button. Wait for the countdown, and then begin stating your math prompt.

5. After you have finished the challenge, tap the "export" button to save the video to your camera roll.

TRY APP SMASHING! Take your video and #AppSmash it into programs like Flipgrid for group collaboration or Seesaw for parent involvement.

REAL LIFE REPLICA

DESCRIPTION

Infuse the traditional student diorama project with the fun effects of green screen video by allowing the student to "walk through" their finished project to deliver a one-of-a-kind presentation!

ISTE STANDARDS

- Students create original works or responsibly repurpose or remix digital resources into new creations. (6b)
- Students publish or present content to customize the message and medium for their intended audiences. (6d)

LESSON SUMMARY

- Students create the diorama per teacher objectives and design. For best video quality, students should try to avoid using the color green as much as possible.
- When the diorama is complete, set it in a well-lit area and take a picture of it. The photo should be taken from above the project and show the project in its entirety.
- Tap the "+" sign on the bottom layer and then tap "image." The student will then select and upload the picture of the project from the camera roll.
- After this, the student will record her video as she "tours" through her own created diorama. She can walk through various spaces and even sit down to explain specific details.
- When filming and video editing is complete, the student will save and download her unique project presentation to the iPad camera roll by tapping the "export" button.

GRADE LEVEL: 3rd-5th

CONTENT AREA(S): Reading, Science, Social Studies

COMFORT LEVEL: Medium

LESSON FORMAT: Student Created

QUICK TIP: Leave enough space for recording so the student can sit, walk, and move freely on the green screen.

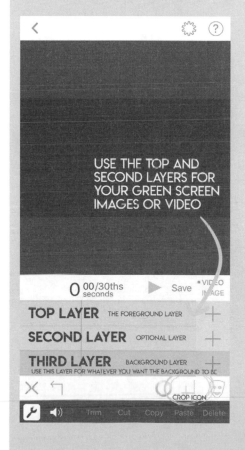

USE THE TOP AND SECOND LAYERS FOR YOUR GREEN SCREEN IMAGES OR VIDEO

0 00/30ths seconds   ▶   Save   •VIDEO •IMAGE

TOP LAYER   THE FOREGROUND LAYER   +

SECOND LAYER   OPTIONAL LAYER   +

THIRD LAYER   BACKGROUND LAYER   +
USE THIS LAYER FOR WHATEVER YOU WANT THE BACKGROUND TO BE

✕   ↩   CROP ICON

🔧 ◀))   Trim   Cut   Copy   Paste   Delete

BECOME A METEOROLOGIST

GRADE LEVEL: Any

CONTENT AREA(S): Science

COMFORT LEVEL: Medium

LESSON FORMAT: Teacher or Student Created

QUICK TIP: Use a tripod when recording so students can see themselves and position where they are standing based on the weather video layered behind them.

DESCRIPTION

Students become a weather meteorologist in minutes as they create a forecast based on local or state weather or on specific forms of severe weather.

ISTE STANDARDS

- Educator will design authentic learning activities to align with content area standards and use digital tools and resources to maximize active, deep learning. (5b)

- Educator will provide alternative ways for students to demonstrate competency and reflect on their learning using technology. (7a)

- Students choose the appropriate platforms and tools for meeting the desired objectives of their creation or communication. (6a)

- Students communicate complex ideas clearly and effectively by creating or using a variety of digital objects such as visualizations, models, or simulations. (6c)

LESSON SUMMARY

1. Begin by finding the images or videos to be used in the forecasting video. You can find and save still images to the camera roll or take a screen recording of the local or state weather channel's highlight reel.

2. Open Do Ink Green Screen and tap on the bottom "+" sign. Ask students to arrange the still images or video clips as needed. Make sure to arrange all the images and clips back to back in the desired order.

3. Ask each student to stand in front of the green screen and record his video directly within the program. To do so, tap the middle layer "+" sign. This will allow him to see the weather images behind him as he is speaking.

4. Edit, clip, or re-record video until the project is ready to save and download to the iPad camera roll.

Schoolwide Sharing: Setting up a green screen booth or activity is a fun and easy way to share the science of green screen with parents. Perhaps include a back-to-school photo station or create a fun weather forecasting booth at the yearly parent night!

Get Started Now! Save these images to your camera roll and start filming your own weather reports now!

STUCK IN A SNOW GLOBE

GRADE LEVEL: K-2

CONTENT AREA(S): Reading and Writing

COMFORT LEVEL: Beginner

LESSON FORMAT: Teacher or Student Created

QUICK TIP: Use the sizing feature in Do Ink to pinch and resize student photos to ensure they fit into the chosen snow globe photo.

DESCRIPTION

No more of the tedious cutting and gluing of student photographs! Use the magic of Do Ink to instantly place your student inside the favorite holiday trademark—the snow globe!

ISTE STANDARDS

- Students communicate complex ideas clearly and effectively by creating or using a variety of digital objects such as visualizations, models, or simulations. (6c)

- Educator will explore and apply instructional design principles to create innovative digital learning environments to engage and support learning. (5c)

- Educator will model and nurture creativity and creative expression to communicate ideas, knowledge, or connections. (6d)

LESSON SUMMARY

1. Students take a photograph of themselves in the position they wish to be in when they are "stuck" in the snow globe and save it to the camera roll. For best picture quality, students should try to avoid wearing the color green as much as possible.

2. Open Do Ink Green Screen and place the snow globe image on the bottom layer by tapping the "+" sign and then selecting "image." Find the saved photo and tap it.

3. Tap the middle layer "+" sign and select "image." Find the picture of your student's green-screened position and select it.

4. Tap the middle layer with the student photo and then tap the "crop" icon. Arrange the constraints until it fits inside the photo of the snow globe.

5. Tap "image" in the upper tool bar. Tap "capture image" to save to the camera roll

"*My students enjoy sharing video presentations with green screens showing different backdrops in the background, depending on what they were highlighting. Creativity is an art. It does not need to be on paper, and it does not need to happen the same way for all of the students for the same project.*"

—Gloriann Heikes (@MrsHeikes)

Tip: Try combining this fun photography with a winter-inspired writing piece!

Get Started Now! Save these images to your camera roll, and you're all set to get stuck in a snow globe!

STANDING IN A STORY

GRADE LEVEL: Any

CONTENT AREA(S): Reading

COMFORT LEVEL: Beginner

LESSON FORMAT: Student Created

QUICK TIP: Take your time to get a good photo of the pages from the story book with as little shadow as possible.

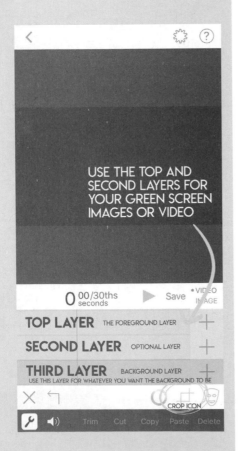

DESCRIPTION

Students can now interact with a story like never before by jumping into the pages of the story to add to their content objectives, such as identifying plot, summarizing, inferring, or analyzing characters.

ISTE STANDARDS

- Students communicate complex ideas clearly and effectively by creating or using a variety of digital objects, such as visualizations, models, or simulations. (6c)

- Students publish or present content to customize the message and medium for their intended audiences. (6d)

LESSON SUMMARY

1. Students take photos of the needed story illustrations to correspond with the specific content area standard they are working on (*ie*, summarization, tracing a character's emotions, plot development, use of pictures in a story, details supporting theme, etc.).

2. To pick the background image, tap on the bottom layer "+" sign, and then select "image." Multiple photos may be used, and the student can order the images the way they want.

3. Students can video record using the camera app or directly through the Do Ink app. Video needs to be recorded or uploaded to the middle layer on the platform by tapping the "+" sign, and then tapping "camera" (within Do Ink) or "video" (if recorded using the camera app).

4. The student can crop, edit, cut, resize, etc. until his recording is complete. Once finished, it can be downloaded to the iPad camera roll by tapping the "export" button.

TRY APP SMASHING!

Take your video and #AppSmash it into programs like Apple Clips. Use the different sketch filters to create the effect of being drawn into a story book.

Tips: To maximize resources and minimize prep time, before the lesson, take photos of all the illustrations in the book and up-load them to a place where students can access them (a drive, loaded on student devices, etc.). This will let students begin their projects right away instead of taking time to find the illustrations they need.

MYSTERY REVEAL

GRADE LEVEL: K-5th

CONTENT AREA(S): Any

COMFORT LEVEL: Medium

LESSON FORMAT: Teacher or Student Created

QUICK TIP: This lesson requires the use of a green writing utensil. A thick green marker works best, but crayons also do the job!

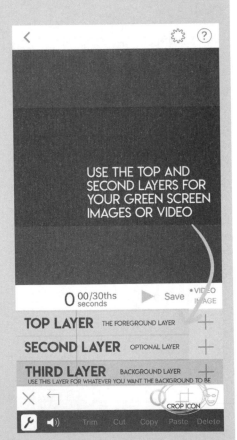

DESCRIPTION

Close out a week's worth of reading with this thrilling mystery reveal activity! Build excitement throughout the week, and use this culminating activity to thoroughly engage your students.

ISTE STANDARDS

- Educator will explore and apply instructional design principles to create innovative digital learning environments to engage and support learning. (5c)

- Students create original works or responsibly repurpose or remix digital resources into new creations. (6b)

THE HOW

1. After reading your selected text, decide what you want the mystery reveal to be. This could be a math equation, main idea statement, science observation, etc.

2. After picking your mystery reveal topic or image, create a slide in PowerPoint or Google Slides containing either the picture or text of your mystery reveal. Save this slide as a jpg file on your camera roll. You could also take a photo of what will be revealed, as long as it ends up on the camera roll.

3. Open Do Ink Green Screen and tap the "+" sign on the bottom layer. Select "image," and tap your jpg file.

4. Tap the middle "+" button and then tap "camera." This will appear to do nothing, but this is where the green markers come in.

5. While one student (or a tripod) holds the camera on the page, ask another student to start scribbling on the white paper with a green marker. This will slowly reveal what is hidden on the middle layer—your mystery reveal! The secret is out!

EXPLORE ENDLESS WAYS TO RECORD

RECOMMENDED TOOLS

Eliminate the excess background noise with a simple and inexpensive microphone like this one! Clip-on microphones are great for allowing multiple student recordings in the classroom simultaneously.

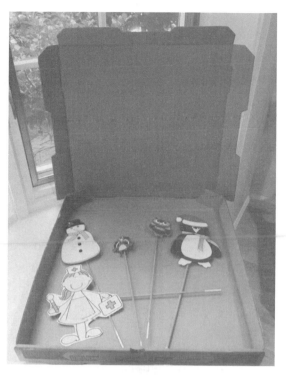

Using a tripod is a great way to free up the students' hands and gives them the opportunity to record independently.

Tripods allow students to be hands-free while recording, while also keeping the video steady and focused.

 WANT TO CONNECT?
Twitter: @DoInkTweets
Website: doink.com
Instagram: Doinkapps
Email: Support@doink.com

BUNCEE

WHAT IS IT?

Buncee is a creation tool fostering communication through its easy-to-use, all-in-one platform. It allows students, teachers, and administrators to create and share visual presentations easily.

WHERE CAN I USE IT?

Buncee is a web-based solution and can be utilized from all devices. The Buncee app can be downloaded in Apple's App Store and at the Microsoft Store.

HOW DOES IT WORK?

Students can start with a blank slide or presentation or choose from thousands of templates. Buncee even allows administration to upload custom templates for their own school or district. Students can create and add over fifteen forms of media to their presentations, including text, video, and animation. Administration can monitor user work and set permissions and privacies schoolwide to ensure the needs of all students are met. It is important to note that Buncee is COPPA compliant and is a signatory of the Student Privacy Pledge, which makes the platform a safe and secure place for students to work.

HOW CAN I USE IT IN THE CLASSROOM?

Students all learn in different ways and at different paces. Buncee offers multiple ways to help students visualize, voice, and communicate their learning—helping build their confidence and engagement. Buncee can be used to create reports, presentations, newsletters, and book reviews filled with rich media.

Did you know? Buncee has multiple Microsoft integrations, including live-embed into OneNote and easy sharing to Microsoft Teams with the push of a button!

Buncee now has Immersive Reader integrated, which makes a powerful combination for any inclusive classroom! It creates an accessible reading experience that has been proven to enhance reading comprehension for learners.

HIGHLIGHTED FEATURES

3D GRAPHICS: 3D Graphics allow students to dive deep into their learning. Anatomical structures, planets, and more can all be viewed from 360 degrees, helping students understand how those parts work together.

360 IMAGES: 360 Images allow students to virtually travel to any destination. These images are perfect for virtual field trips and exploring different parts of the world.

RECORDED VIDEO: Video recording is a great feature for amplifying student voice (#Stuvoice). Students are able to record a video of themselves without leaving the Buncee platform.

ANIMATIONS: The Buncee library of animated graphics is diverse and always growing. From educational animations explaining complex concepts to fun animations to keep students engaged, an animation is available for almost any project.

DRAWING TOOL: Students can draw directly onto their creation using Buncee's drawing tool. Whether they want to annotate an uploaded photo or draw their own design, the drawing tool can help (on iOS and the web).

FRQ/MCQ: Use the Multiple Choice or Free Response Questions to create assessments and resources for your students. With the Buncee Classroom Dashboard, you can review students' responses, grade, and remark.

WANT TO CONNECT?
Twitter: @Buncee
Website: app.edu.buncee.com
Instagram: Buncee

> *"We make playlists on Buncee with different steps the students are to do while I am working with kids. It creates and fosters a high level of independence and accountability, but it has also opened doors for them to be creative."*
>
> —Sara Frater (@sarafrater)

BUNCEE BENTO BOX

GRADE LEVEL: 3rd-5th

CONTENT AREA(S): Reading

COMFORT LEVEL: Beginner

LESSON FORMAT: Student Created

QUICK TIP: If students are new to using Buncee, try using the Bento Box template!

DESCRIPTION

Book Bentos are a unique and fun way to share book reviews. Think of it as a book recommendation with a photograph of images included in the recommendation!

ISTE STANDARDS

- Students curate information from digital resources using a variety of tools and methods to create collections of artifacts to demonstrate meaningful connections or conclusions. (3c)
- Students communicate complex ideas clearly and effectively by creating or using a variety of digital objects such as visualizations, models, or simulations. (6c)

LESSON SUMMARY

1. After reading a story, the student brainstorms objects related to the story. The student will demonstrate her understanding of the story by choosing significant events or objects related to it.

2. The student begins by opening a new project and placing the photograph of the book cover in the center.

3. The student can then use the media features in Buncee to surround the book with the items she previously brainstormed.

4. Elements such as audio clips can even be added to give the presentation more accessibility.

CHECK OUT A SIMPLE EXAMPLE BENTO BOX ILLUSTRATING
THE STORY *NUMBER THE STARS* BY LOIS LOWRY.

 For some inspiring photos, check out the @bookbento
Instagram feed or check out the #bookbento hashtag!

@BookBento QR code linked to profile

#bookbento QR code linked to feed

STORY PUBLISHING

GRADE LEVEL: Any

CONTENT AREA(S): Writing

COMFORT LEVEL: Beginner

LESSON FORMAT: Student Created

QUICK TIP: Have the students add an audio recording of the text they embed into their Buncee.

DESCRIPTION

Take writing to the next level by publishing final drafts as a Buncee! Then share the Buncees with classmates and families.

ISTE STANDARDS

- Students choose the appropriate platforms and tools for meeting the desired objectives of their creation or communication. (6a)

- Students create original works or responsibly repurpose or remix digital resources into new creations. (6b)

- Students publish or present content that customizes the message and medium for their intended audiences. (6d)

LESSON SUMMARY

1. Ask students to complete a writing task.

2. Once they reach the publishing phase, allow them to design a Buncee.

3. As they work on their Buncee, encourage them to add text, images, animations, or drawings. Students can also add voice recordings in which they read the text they embed.

4. When the Buncee is complete, have the students tap or click the "share" icon to generate either a link or a slide deck image.

TRY APP SMASHING! Take your Buncee and #AppSmash it into programs like Seesaw or Flipgrid. This will allow families to view student work and also generate classroom discussion.

 CHECK OUT AN EXAMPLE HERE!

The knight came back and scared the witch away. If there were any beanstalks left, they would start to shrink. Than came the exciting part. The knight was about to reveal his identity. He took of the mask and it was Nate's neighbor!After,the day went back to normal like nothing even happened. The only difference was some roofs were broken.

It was so cool! We loved it ! We saw so many different animals under the sea!

ALL ABOUT ME

GRADE LEVEL: Any

CONTENT AREA(S): Ice Breaker

COMFORT LEVEL: Beginner

LESSON FORMAT: Student Created

QUICK TIP: Create a "Get to Know Me" Buncee the first week of school. This not only helps students get to know each other but also helps students learn the platform early in the year.

DESCRIPTION

Students get a chance to introduce themselves to their new class through a Buncee filled with media all about them! Having students use Buncee in this way is a great way to teach them how to use the platform in a safe, relaxed environment before classroom content is introduced.

ISTE STANDARDS

- Students communicate complex ideas clearly and effectively by creating or using a variety of digital objects such as visualizations, models, or simulations. (6c)

- Students publish or present content to customize the message and medium for their intended audiences. (6d)

- Students use digital tools to connect with learners from a variety of backgrounds and cultures, engaging with them in ways to broaden mutual understanding and learning. (7a)

LESSON SUMMARY

1. Students start with a blank template or use one of the many pre-created templates.

2. Students can edit and alter the templates and slides, adding video, pictures, and animations about themselves. You may want to give a set of guidelines for students to help them get started and share consistently.

3. When finished, students can share individually in front of the class or, using the "clip and stitch" feature, you can clip all student slides together to create one final class Buncee.

TRY APP SMASHING! Students can take their finished Buncees and #AppSmash them into Flipgrid as one of the ten attachments. There they can add a video introduction for the class along with their created Buncee presentation.

Teacher Twist

Create a Buncee for your Meet the Teacher or Open House and let it loop through while you meet and mingle with your new students and their families!

all about  Mrs. Merrill

I HAVE TWO SONS-AGE 8 AND 5.

I HAVE BEEN TEACHING FOR 11 YEARS.

SMILE

I AM MARRIED TO MR. MERRILL WHO TEACHES FIRST GRADE AT TPE

CHECK OUT AN EXAMPLE OF HOW TO GREET NEW STUDENTS!

INTERACTIVE MATH PROBLEMS

GRADE LEVEL: K-3rd

CONTENT AREA(S): Math

COMFORT LEVEL: Medium

LESSON FORMAT: Teacher Created

QUICK TIP: For easier use, leave images and visuals already set out for students before math time. This way more time is spent on math rather than searching for images.

DESCRIPTION

Help students visualize various math problems using the interactive media features available on Buncee. These activities could be done in class, delivered through centers, or even given as interactive homework!

ISTE STANDARDS

- Educator will design authentic learning activities to align with content area standards and use digital tools and resources to maximize active, deep learning. (5b)

- Educator will explore and apply instructional design principles to create innovative digital learning environments to engage and support learning. (5c)

LESSON SUMMARY

- Create a Buncee slide with math problems relative to your standards.

- You can copy, paste, or duplicate the slide to build more quickly.

- Encourage students to add media (video, drawing, audio recording, etc.) when answering the questions.

- When students are finished, share the Bunce deck with parents.

KAREN IS SHARING THE LAST OF HER CANDY WITH HER THREE FRIENDS. HOW MANY CAN EACH HAVE IF THEY ALL GET THE SAME AMOUNT?

CHECK OUT AN EXAMPLE HERE!

KEEP STUDENTS INVOLVED BY SENDING THIS ACTIVITY HOME FOR EXTRA PRACTICE.

CLASS RULES COLLABORATION

GRADE LEVEL: Any

CONTENT AREA(S): Reading, Writing

COMFORT LEVEL: Beginner

LESSON FORMAT: Student Created

QUICK TIP: To avoid lots of repetition, give groups of students different topics—responsible, respectful, kind, ready to learn—to create rules about. This will give the class a diverse set of student-created rules!

DESCRIPTION

Creating a close classroom environment works best when students are given a choice and a voice within it. Start a class discussion about rules based on a read-aloud. Then give students a chance to brainstorm rules that would be beneficial to follow as a class.

ISTE STANDARDS

- Students create original works or responsibly repurpose or remix digital resources into new creations. (6b)

- Students use collaborative technologies to work with others, including peers, experts, or community members, to examine issues and problems from multiple viewpoints. (7b)

- Students contribute constructively to project teams, assuming various roles and responsibilities to work effectively toward a common goal. (7c)

LESSON SUMMARY

1. Before designing, the teacher should lead the class in a brainstorming session focused on rules. This can be in the form of a class read-aloud or through a mind mapping activity.
2. After the class discussion, students may work individually, in partner pairs, or in groups to start curating their list of essential class rules.
3. Teacher can give guidelines or a checklist of items for each slide and help model design features such as font size and color, background style, and image sizing.

SUGGESTED READ-ALOUDS:

What If Everybody Did That?
by Ellen Javernick

The Worst Day of My Life Ever!
by Julia Cook

Lilly's Purple Plastic Purse
by Kevin Henkes

No David!
by David Shannon

Back to School Rules
by Laurie Friedman

 Tip: Try using the Buncee feature "clip and stitch" to piece together slides from different student Buncees to create one cohesive set of class rules.

Prepare well for the next day

Listen wile the teacher is talking

Remember your homework

 CHECK OUT THE ENTIRE EXAMPLE PRESENTATION HERE!

DIGITAL PORTFOLIOS

GRADE LEVEL: 2nd-5th

CONTENT AREA(S): Assessment/ Data Collection

COMFORT LEVEL: Advanced

LESSON FORMAT: Student Created

QUICK TIP: Teaching students how to take good photos of work and assignments will result in better-quality artifacts.

DESCRIPTION

Document student work throughout the year using Buncee. Students can upload photos of student work, record reflections, and curate their progress for the school year.

ISTE STANDARDS

- Students curate information from digital resources using a variety of tools and methods to create collections of artifacts to demonstrate meaningful connections or conclusions. (3c)

- Students collect data or identify relevant data sets, use digital tools to analyze them, and represent data in various ways to facilitate problem-solving and decision-making. (5b)

- Students publish or present content to customize the message and medium for their intended audiences. (6d)

LESSON SUMMARY

1. Give students time to create their own Buncee entitled "Portfolio." Allow students to design it as they see fit and create it in a way to represent themselves.

2. As the year progresses, ask the students to upload completed tasks to their Buncee. These can be an image, video, recording, etc.

3. When the students have enough artifacts uploaded, tap or click the "share" icon. This allows you to generate either an image or a direct link.

4. Share with families at the end of the year or—even better— share the link early in the year so they can check in and follow along with their students as they continually add artifacts.

WORLDLY WRITING

DESCRIPTION

Write your way through history as you "travel" to different places, historical events, or famous geographical locations. Allow students to show what they know through creative writing.

ISTE STANDARDS

- Students publish or present content to customize the message and medium for their intended audiences. (6d)

LESSON SUMMARY

1. Using Buncee templates of a postcard and travel passport, you can either assign a premade Buncee to your class or assist students in finding the already-made templates.

2. Depending on the lesson, students take time toward the end of the lesson or unit to write about what they've learned in first-person format.

3. Students write about their "experience," share what they've learned, and express their point of view through the post cards.

4. The passport template is a fun addition to the writing; students can find fun stamps to represent their "travels" or photographs to match the topics they have written about.

Buncee templates work great for this writing lesson! Students can write and add photos to document their "travels."

GRADE LEVEL: 3rd-5th

CONTENT AREA(S): Reading, Writing, History

COMFORT LEVEL: Beginner

LESSON FORMAT: Student Created

QUICK TIP: If students' typing skills are not fully developed, ask them to dictate their words using the dictation tool on the iPad.

POETRY PRACTICE CENTERS

GRADE LEVEL: 3rd-5th

CONTENT AREA(S): Reading

COMFORT LEVEL: Medium

LESSON FORMAT: Teacher Created

QUICK TIP: For best practice, students should use this type of center after reviewing elements of poetry together as a class.

DESCRIPTION

Create independent, student-paced centers focused on a weekly poem. This is a great way to focus on figurative language and all things poetry-related in a fun and interactive format.

ISTE STANDARDS

- Educator will use technology to create, adapt, and personalize learning experiences to foster independent learning and accommodate learner differences and needs. (5a)

- Educator will design authentic learning activities to align with content area standards and use digital tools and resources to maximize active, deep learning. (5b)

- Educator will foster a culture where students take ownership of their learning goals and outcomes in both independent and group settings. (6a)

LESSON SUMMARY

1. Start with the selected poem you wish to have students read and analyze throughout the week. This can be added to the first slide of the weekly Buncee, but giving students a paper copy is also nice so students can refer to it regardless of the slide they are working on.

2. Create a slide (or more!) for each day with the various activities you want the class to work on. Don't be afraid to use various tools (like drawing) to give students various tasks.

3. When finished, assign the Buncee to the intended students. When completed, students can turn in the assignment for you to review.

Tip: This lesson is a great way to differentiate for the needs of learners. Create one assignment for all students, but with each student receiving a different poem. Or, assign various Buncees to groups according to their specific learning goals.

Give students a poem each week, asking them to revisit it with a new focus each day.

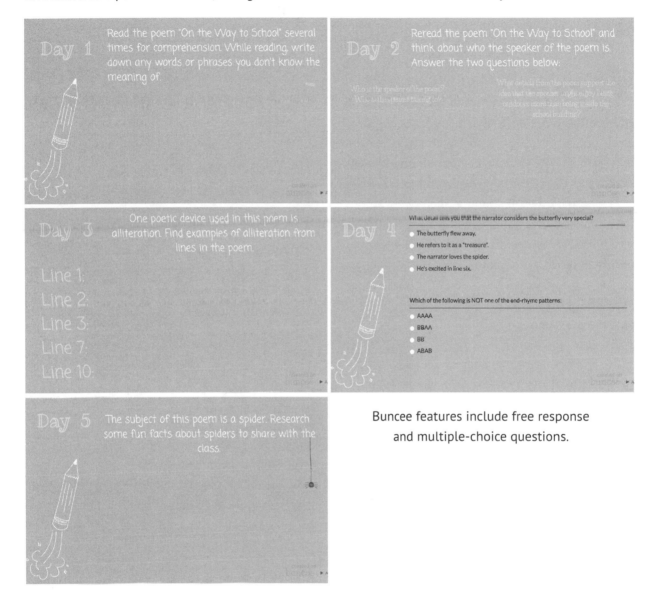

Buncee features include free response and multiple-choice questions.

 Tip: Try assigning weekly centers with other things besides poetry. Daily writing warmups or math word problems could work with the same format.

CLASS

SEESAW

WHAT IS IT?

Seesaw is a platform for students to demonstrate and share their understanding. Students use powerful tools in the Seesaw app to create, reflect on, and demonstrate learning. Information is safely saved and formed into a digital portfolio. When students share their learning in their Seesaw portfolio, teachers and families gain valuable insights into what the students know and can better support their development throughout the school year.

WHERE CAN I USE IT?

Seesaw is available on all major platforms. There are several pricing options ranging from free to $120. The free version of Seesaw will provide educators with all the basic features, permit one hundred activities, connect two teachers per class, and enable each teacher to have up to ten classes.

Seesaw Plus features all the above with the ability to schedule activities, have up to twenty-five classes, permit five hundred activities, add recorded private notes on student work, and assess student progress toward skills and standards.

HOW DOES IT WORK?

Teachers can use Seesaw as a place for students to share their work and to encourage individual reflection and peer feedback. Seesaw becomes a place not only where student work can be stored, but where teachers and peers can provide encouragement, constructive criticism, and suggestions for improvement. Teachers have the opportunity to review any comments before they are posted to ensure feedback is constructive and appropriate.

Teachers can also seek out activities and assignments in the Activity Library. Here, teachers can find grade level–specific content to use immediately.

When shared, families only see *their* child's work and can leave comments and encouragement. This is a great way for teachers to provide a window into their classrooms.

HOW CAN I USE IT IN THE CLASSROOM?

Students can add images, video, audio, files, or notes. They can even annotate over a picture from their device. For example, students can work out a math problem on a whiteboard, take a picture of their work, and then upload it to Seesaw. Once the image is uploaded, they can annotate over the image by adding an audio recording of themselves explaining their thinking.

Students, teachers, and families can all comment on artifacts using text or voice comments. This provides meaningful feedback from all parties and encourages students to do their best.

Teachers have the ability to create folders for assignments. This is beneficial during conferences, for example, where the teacher can quickly open particular subjects. When teachers create an assignment, they have the ability to share activities with the rest of their team.

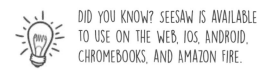

DID YOU KNOW? SEESAW IS AVAILABLE TO USE ON THE WEB, IOS, ANDROID, CHROMEBOOKS, AND AMAZON FIRE.

HIGHLIGHTED FEATURES

MULTIMEDIA: Students can add images, video, audio, files, or notes. In some cases, they can add more than one of these at once. For example, a student can draw and record an audio excerpt explaining their thinking.

VIEW INSTRUCTIONS: While completing an assignment, students can tap "view instructions" to go back and make sure they are completing the task correctly.

INSERTING SHAPES AND BACKGROUNDS: Students are able to easily add shapes and background images while drawing or annotating on top of them.

CAPTIONS: Students can add text or audio captions.

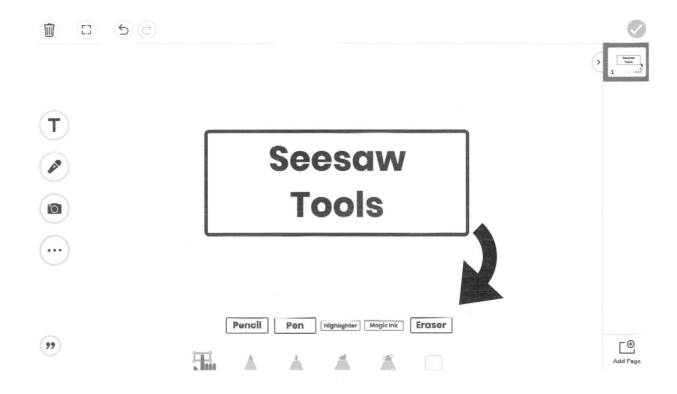

WANT TO CONNECT?
Twitter: @Seesaw
Website: web.seesaw.me
Instagram: @seesawlearning

DOT TALKS

GRADE LEVEL: K-2nd

CONTENT AREA(S): Math

COMFORT LEVEL: Beginner

LESSON FORMAT: Teacher Created, Student Edited

QUICK TIP: This assignment could be altered to be "Number Talks," where you just display a number rather than images of dots.

DESCRIPTION

Dot Talks is a quick, fun, and engaging way to encourage critical thinking in mental math. For example, using Seesaw's features, students look at the assigned number of dots. They circle *some* of the dots but not all of them. Then they can explain how the number of circled dots plus the number of uncircled dots adds up to the grand total of dots. Finally, they explain their thinking.

ISTE STANDARDS

- Students know and use a deliberate design process for generating ideas, testing theories, creating innovative artifacts, or solving authentic problems. (4a)
- Students select and use digital tools to plan and manage a design process to consider design constraints and calculated risks. (4b)

LESSON SUMMARY

1. Scan the QR Code to download our Dot Talks template for PowerPoint or Google Slides (or create your own).

2. If you're using our template, you can copy and paste the dots included. If you're using your own template, insert the total number of dots.

3. Open Seesaw and tap or click on the green "+" sign.

4. Tap or click on "Browse Activity Library," then tap or click "My Library" on the top left of your screen.

5. Tap or click "Create New Activity," and give your activity a name in the top box. Since Dot Talks could be a recurring activity, you might want to name the activity "Dot Talks #___," with the underscore being the total number of dots.

6. Next, add directions for your students. For this activity, we recommend: "Circle a few of the dots, but NOT all. Write the number of dots you circled and the number of dots left. Then create an equation and add up the two numbers to see how many dots there are altogether."

7. You have the option to add voice instructions, too. We recommend this when assigning to younger students.

8. Tap or click on "Add Template for Student Responses."

9. Upload the Dot Talks template with your dots inserted. The students will complete the task using this template.

10. When ready, tap the blue "Save" button on the bottom right side of your screen.

11. To share the activity with your class, tap or click the green "Share" button, then select the appropriate class.

12. Tap or click on the green "Share with 1 Class" button to assign to your students.

WANT TO TRY THIS TODAY? DOWNLOAD OUR FREE EDITABLE TEMPLATE BY SCANNING THE QR CODE!

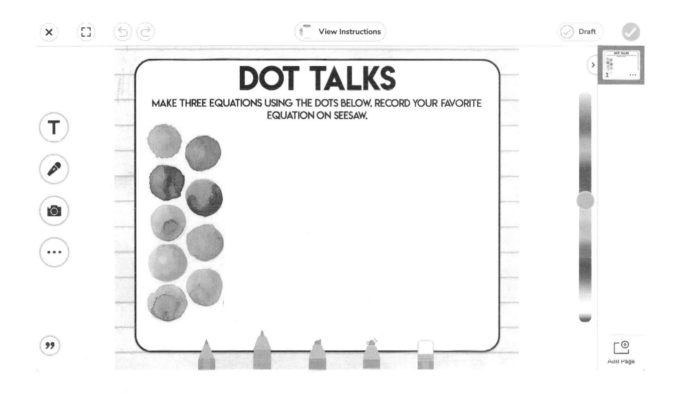

IN OR OUT?

GRADE LEVEL: K-3rd

CONTENT AREA(S): Reading, Math, Science

COMFORT LEVEL: Beginner

LESSON FORMAT: Teacher Created

QUICK TIP: You can use Seesaw codes to add icons to the directions. For example, using the code ":mic:" will display a microphone icon. Use this feature when assigning this activity to younger students.

DESCRIPTION

Develop critical thinking in your students by giving them a chance to explain their thinking and create friendly controversy.

ISTE STANDARDS

- Students use digital tools to connect with learners from a variety of backgrounds and cultures, engaging with them in ways that broaden mutual understanding and learning. (7a)

- Students use collaborative technologies to work with others, including peers, experts, or community members, to examine issues and problems from multiple viewpoints. (7b)

LESSON SUMMARY

1. Scan the QR Code to download our "In or Out" template for PowerPoint or Google Slides (or create your own).

2. Add four new images you would like your students to compare, then save the file. For example, if you insert an image of Oreos, chocolate chip cookies, sugar cookies, and oatmeal cookies, students might suggest the Oreos should be *out* because they're the only one with filling. Other students might disagree and suggest the sugar cookies should be *out* because they don't have an extra ingredient mixed in.

3. Open Seesaw and tap or click on the green "+" sign.

4. Tap or click on "Browse Activity Library," then tap or click "My Library" on the top left of your screen.

5. Tap or click "Create New Activity," and give your activity a name in the top box.

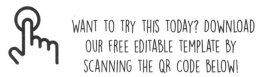

WANT TO TRY THIS TODAY? DOWNLOAD OUR FREE EDITABLE TEMPLATE BY SCANNING THE QR CODE BELOW!

6. Add directions for your students. For this activity, we recommend: "Look at the images in the four squares. Which image does not belong? Use the microphone tool to record your thinking."

7. You have the option to add voice instructions, too. We recommend this when assigning to younger students.

8. Tap or click on "Add Template for Student Responses."

9. Upload the "In or Out" template with your images inserted. The students will complete the task with this.

10. When ready, tap the blue "Save" button on the bottom right side of your screen.

11. To share the activity with your class, tap or click on the green "Share" button and then select the appropriate class.

12. Tap or click on the green "Share with 1 Class" button to assign to your students.

ALL ABOUT ME

GRADE LEVEL: K-5th

CONTENT AREA(S): Reading

COMFORT LEVEL: Beginner

LESSON FORMAT: Student Created

QUICK TIP: When adding the text boxes, change the background from being transparent to having a color. This will make it easier to read.

DESCRIPTION

This is a great way for students to introduce themselves to one another while you teach them tech. In "All about Me," your students take a selfie in Seesaw and then add text boxes, using adjectives they feel best describe themselves.

ISTE STANDARDS

- Students publish or present content to customize the message and medium for their intended audiences. (6d)

LESSON SUMMARY

1. On Seesaw or in the app, the students tap or click on the green "+" sign.

2. Tap or click on "Add to Student Journal."

3. Tap or click on "Photo" and take the selfie.

4. Tap or click on the "T" icon (text box) to add adjectives to describe themselves. Repeat this step as needed.

5. When finished, tap or click on the green check mark in the upper right corner to submit.

THE #INTERACTIVE CLASS @THEMERRILLSEDU

USE THIS SPACE FOR SKETCH NOTES, IDEAS, ETC!

TEXTING STORY

WHAT IS IT?

Texting Story is an app to allow the user to create a fake text messaging thread. Users can easily switch characters, add emojis, and export the conversation as a video to the camera roll.

WHERE CAN I USE IT?

Texting Story is an app compatible with both iOS and Android devices. It is not available on the web.

HOW DOES IT WORK?

Creating a conversation thread in Texting Story is easy! Create two character names by tapping on the names at the top. Easily toggle back and forth between the two characters to generate a conversation. Texting Story records each keystroke but will automatically speed up the conversation when exporting the clip. After previewing, export the clip into a video and save it to the camera roll.

HOW CAN I USE IT IN THE CLASSROOM?

Conversations created through Texting Story can be integrated into multiple subject areas. Students can compare and contrast characters, draw conclusions based on people's and characters' emotions, and make predictions in a story or before learning about a historical event. Conversations can be in third person, between two people, or taking place as a first-person conversation between a student and a fictional character or historical person.

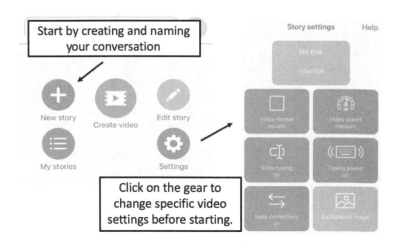

Start by creating and naming your conversation

Click on the gear to change specific video settings before starting.

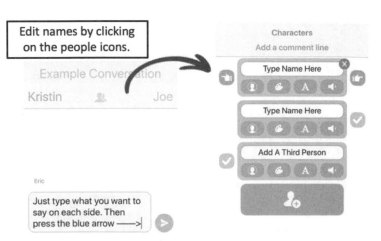

Edit names by clicking on the people icons.

Take your video and #AppSmash it into programs like Flipgrid. Generate a classroom discussion in which students can share their comparisons and conversations.

TEXTING STORY TEMPLATE

NAME:_____ DATE:_____

CREATE A TEXT MESSAGE BETWEEN TWO CHARACTERS AND DESCRIBE THEIR FEELINGS IN THE BEGINNING, MIDDLE AND END.

B = BLUE CHARACTER   O = ORANGE CHARACTER

Get Started Now! Download the simple template for students to plan their conversations before typing.

CONVERSATION WITH COLUMBUS

GRADE LEVEL: 3rd-5th

CONTENT AREA(S): History

COMFORT LEVEL: Beginner

LESSON FORMAT: Student Created

QUICK TIP: This is a fun activity to create engagement and evaluate student understanding when analyzing historical documents within a unit.

DESCRIPTION

Using information to infer is fun when you do it through a modern-day conversational text. This lesson can be used in almost any history lesson or unit and sparks lots of conversations and critical thinking.

ISTE STANDARDS

- Students communicate complex ideas clearly and effectively by creating or using a variety of digital objects such as visualizations, models, or simulations. (6c)

- Students publish or present content to customize the message and medium for their intended audiences. (6d)

- Students use collaborative technologies to work with others, including peers, experts, or community members, to examine issues and problems from multiple viewpoints. (7b)

LESSON SUMMARY

1. Within a unit of study, take time as a class to analyze a historical document, painting, etc.

2. Give students time to make observations that then lead to support inferences.

3. Ask students to create a conversation between people (or objects) within the document based on inferred observations.

4. Save the Texting Story project as a video on the device's camera roll.

CHECK OUT THIS AMAZING CONVERSATION BETWEEN QUEEN ISABELLA AND CHRISTOPHER COLUMBUS!

Columbus 👥 Queen

Can I go on a journey?

Well if you do tell me where you want to go and what you want to do.

I want to explore a new route to Asia and find gold.

Fine. But if you go in my

Message

Columbus 👥 Queen

name you must return successful.

I promise to do my best.

You are going to need some things to help you on your journey.

Like what?

Message

Columbus 👥 Queen

Well first off you're going to need a ship to travel on.

You will take the Nina, Pinta and the Santa Maria.

Wow! Thank you so much!

Message

CONCLUDING CONVERSATIONS

GRADE LEVEL: Any

CONTENT AREA(S): Reading

COMFORT LEVEL: Beginner

LESSON FORMAT: Teacher Created

QUICK TIP: Try embedding emojis in place of words to encourage creative thinking!

DESCRIPTION

Encourage higher-level thinking with this fun and subjective reading activity! Create a fictitious conversation for students to analyze and draw conclusions throughout.

ISTE STANDARDS

- Educator will explore and apply instructional design principles to create innovative digital learning environments to engage and support learning. (5c)
- Educator will model and nurture creativity and creative expression to communicate ideas, knowledge, or connections. (6d)

LESSON SUMMARY

1. Open the Texting Story app and generate a new discussion between two characters. Picking characters who are in conflict is helpful.

2. Generate a conversation between two characters in Texting Story. These can be characters from a story or real people at school (e.g., principal, librarian, reading coach, etc.).

3. Create dialogue in the conversation, leaving clues for students, but not giving the solution outright.

4. Save the Texting Story project as a video on the device's camera roll. Then use the mock conversation with students in class.

Take your video and #AppSmash it into programs like Flipgrid. Generate a classroom discussion in which students can discuss their thoughts and share their inferences with each other.

 CHECK OUT MR. MERRILL'S CONCLUSION CONVERSATION!

textingstory.com

Assistant Principal Principal

Someone took the donut off my desk!

I know!

Did anyone walk by my office?

Message

CHARTING CHARACTER EMOTIONS

GRADE LEVEL: Any

CONTENT AREA(S): Reading

COMFORT LEVEL: Beginner

LESSON FORMAT: Student Created

QUICK TIP: Have the students plan out their thinking on a recording sheet before creating a Texting Story video.

DESCRIPTION

Describe the characters' emotions and trace them throughout the text. Then create a fake text messaging thread using Texting Story!

ISTE STANDARDS

- Students communicate complex ideas clearly and effectively by creating or using a variety of digital objects such as visualizations, models, or simulations. (6c)

- Students publish or present content to customize the message and medium for their intended audiences. (6d)

LESSON SUMMARY

1. Begin this lesson after reading a picture book or short story with your class.

2. Using a recording sheet, ask students to brainstorm adjectives describing the emotions of the character(s) in the beginning, middle, and end of the story.

3. Using another recording sheet, ask students to come up with a "fake" text messaging thread between two characters at different parts in the plotline.

4. Using Texting Story, ask students to create their text messaging thread.

5. Save the Texting Story project as a video on the device's camera roll.

THE #INTERACTIVE CLASS @THEMERRILLSEDU

USE THIS SPACE FOR SKETCH NOTES, IDEAS, ETC!

CHATTERPIX KIDS

WHAT IS IT?

ChatterPix Kids is user-friendly and appropriate for kids of all ages, but particularly great to use with the youngest learners in kindergarten and first grade. ChatterPix Kids, a subsidiary of Khan Academy, is a free animation app. Perfect for younger students, it doesn't use ads or subscriptions. With ChatterPix Kids, students can easily create basic animations, bringing photos to life.

WHERE CAN I USE IT?

ChatterPix, one of many applications from Duck Duck Moose, can be downloaded for free from the iOS or Google Play store.

HOW DOES IT WORK?

Simply take any photo, draw a line to make a mouth, and record your voice. Share your Pix with friends and family as silly greetings, playful messages, creative cards, or even fancy book reports. Students have up to thirty seconds to record a message before adding stickers or applying filters. Video clips can be downloaded to devices, which then gives users the option to share on other platforms, including but not limited to Flipgrid, Seesaw, Wakelet, and more!

HOW CAN I USE IT IN THE CLASSROOM?

Students can use images they save from the web, cartoon images within the app, or they can take their own photos of things to animate and voice over. Students can use this to record quick book reviews, animated character recaps, math problem explanations, and more!

WANT TO CONNECT?
Twitter: @ChatterPixIt
Website: duckduckmoose.com
Instagram: #chatterpix or
@Duckduckmooseapps

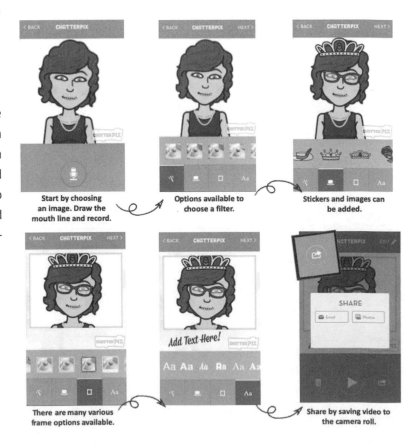

Start by choosing an image. Draw the mouth line and record.

Options available to choose a filter.

Stickers and images can be added.

There are many various frame options available.

Add Text Here!

SHARE

Share by saving video to the camera roll.

ONE WORD SUMMARY

DESCRIPTION

Summarizing is a powerful strategy and should be incorporated into everyone's teaching practice. Give students a chance to brainstorm, draw, and explain a concept through this fun exit ticket activity.

ISTE STANDARDS

- Students create original works or responsibly repurpose or remix digital resources into new creations. (6b)
- Students publish or present content to customize the message and medium for their intended audiences. (6d)

LESSON SUMMARY

- Students begin by choosing one word to summarize the lesson or unit. This word should reflect the main idea of the lesson, story, or activity.
- Students draw illustrations to "decorate" and show the word's meaning.
- Using ChatterPix Kids, students take a photo of their illustrated word and animate it by drawing a "mouth" on it.
- Students record a thirty-second-or-less explanation of why they chose this word to summarize the main idea of the lesson.
- Using the "sharrow", students save their video clip to the camera roll. From here they can share with the class per teacher directions.

GRADE LEVEL: Any

CONTENT AREA(S): Any

COMFORT LEVEL: Beginner

LESSON FORMAT: Student Created

QUICK TIP: As a class, try to brainstorm a list of words students can choose from.

BOOK COVER CHAT

GRADE LEVEL: Any

CONTENT AREA(S): Reading

COMFORT LEVEL: Beginner

LESSON FORMAT: Student Created

QUICK TIP: Create a grid in Flipgrid with topics for each genre and have students upload their book reviews to the appropriate topic for curated book reviews by genre!

TRY APP SMASHING!

#AppSmash with Flipgrid to create interactive videos using the new Flipgrid AR feature!

DESCRIPTION

Try this creative twist on book reports or reviews geared specifically for younger learners by using ChatterPix Kids.

ISTE STANDARDS

- Students choose the appropriate platforms and tools for meeting the desired objectives of their creation or communication. (6a)

LESSON SUMMARY

1. After reading (picture book, story, novel), students take a picture of the novel and upload it to ChatterPix Kids.

2. Students draw the mouth in a position to make it look like the book is talking. Eyes can be added by using the "stickers" feature.

3. Teacher can have students respond to multiple topics, including:

   - Main idea of a story
   - Theme of a story
   - Importance of an integral setting
   - Plot line of the story
   - Character conflict(s)
   - Justifying a title for the story
   - Change in character or setting over time

4. When finished, ask students to download the video and share it with the class.

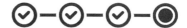

SEQUENCE OF EVENTS

DESCRIPTION

Checking your students' understanding of the text and having them explain the sequence of events can be fun! Have them use ChatterPix Kids to bring the text to life!

ISTE STANDARDS

- Students use technology to seek feedback to inform and improve their practice and to demonstrate their learning in a variety of ways. (1c)

- Students understand the fundamental concepts of technology operations, demonstrate the ability to choose, use, and troubleshoot current technologies, and are able to transfer their knowledge to explore emerging technologies. (1d)

- Students choose the appropriate platforms and tools for meeting the desired objectives of their creation or communication. (6a)

LESSON SUMMARY

1. Read a book aloud and stop at various points in the text to ask questions and monitor for comprehension.

2. After reading, give each student a sheet of blank white paper.

3. Have the students fold the paper into thirds.

4. In each section, the students can draw a picture of one of the main characters in the beginning, middle, and end of the story. It's helpful to label each of them.

5. On ChatterPix Kids, students tap "take a photo," and capture an image of each drawing they created.

6. Using the beginning image, students will slide the dotted line to the right to make a mouth, which will then become animated.

7. Next, students record a thirty-second audio clip, explaining the character at the beginning of the story.

8. Repeat this step twice more to create video clips for the middle and ending as well.

9. Export the video and save it to the Camera Roll.

GRADE LEVEL: Any

CONTENT AREA(S): Reading

COMFORT LEVEL: Beginner

LESSON FORMAT: Student Created

QUICK TIP: Having students write their ideas on paper before recording will help students be more time efficient and organized.

TRY APP SMASHING!

Have the students #AppSmash each video into programs like Apple Clips. There they can drop all three video clips together and make it into one longer video, which could then be shared in programs like Seesaw or Flipgrid.

COMMUNICATING CHARACTERS' PERSPECTIVES

GRADE LEVEL: Any

CONTENT AREA(S): Reading

COMFORT LEVEL: Beginner

LESSON FORMAT: Teacher and Student Created

QUICK TIP: This lesson works best with a book with lots of characters and viewpoints.

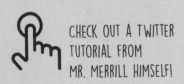

CHECK OUT A TWITTER TUTORIAL FROM MR. MERRILL HIMSELF!

DESCRIPTION

Easily generate a classroom discussion about the characters' perspectives in a text. What were the lessons learned? How did they feel? All of this can be integrated into ChatterPix Kids, where your students can share their thinking.

ISTE STANDARDS

- Students understand the fundamental concepts of technology operations, demonstrate the ability to choose, use, and troubleshoot current technologies, and are able to transfer their knowledge to explore emerging technologies. (1d)

- Students know and use a deliberate design process for generating ideas, testing theories, creating innovative artifacts, or solving authentic problems. (4a)

LESSON SUMMARY

1. Read a book aloud and discuss the various characters' feelings throughout the text.

2. After reading, have a PowerPoint slide with the characters displayed on the board.

3. Allow the students to take a picture of a character of their choice.

4. Open the picture in ChatterPix Kids and animate the character by recording a short audio message describing the lessons learned from the story, an event from their point of view, or any prompt you choose.

5. Repeat as necessary.

TRY APP SMASHING! Place a picture of each character on Flipgrid ahead of time. Have the students respond to the picture of the character they chose. This keeps an organized thread and generates a classroom discussion.

THE
#INTERACTIVE CLASS @THEMERRILLSEDU
USE THIS SPACE FOR SKETCH NOTES, IDEAS, ETC!

GOOGLE SLIDES

ONLINE PLATFORM: Google Slides does not require any particular setup or driver installation to get started. You can start working on your presentation by logging into your Google account.

COLLABORATION: Google Slides allows multiple users to work simultaneously on the same project, contributing their knowledge from different fields. Tracking changes, allowing version control, and adding a conversational interface provides powerful collaboration tools to users who want to chat during the creative process.

MOBILE READY: Google Slides is designed to work on any platform, including mobile devices.

PHOTO EDITING AND MASKING FEATURE: Editing your photos in Google Slides with Recolor and using Photo Masking will help your slide images stand out.

FONTS ENGINE: Google's font library engine, embedded into Google Slides, helps users sort through fonts efficiently.

INSERT GOOGLE SLIDES INTO GOOGLE DOCS: This feature allows you to easily embed your Google Slides into your Google Docs. Furthermore, the files will sync automatically. So, if you make a change on your Google Slide deck, the changes will be reflected (without having to update) in the Google Doc.

POWERPOINT

DESIGNER: The Designer feature, using AI, allows you to create professional slide layouts. Designer is inclusive because people with disabilities can easily use it; without it they might not be able to create with the same level of detail. Read more here!

REAL-TIME CAPTIONS AND TRANSLATION: This feature makes your presentations more inclusive. It is now available for Desktop, Mac, and Web. Read more here!

RECORDING VIDEO WITH NARRATION AND TIMINGS: PowerPoint makes screen recordings easy with this built-in and easy-to-use feature. Read more here!

MICROSOFT FORMS INTEGRATION: PowerPoint allows you to embed a form into your document for people to fill out. Read more here!

MORPH: This feature allows you to make fluid and amazing transitions easily. The Morph transition allows you to animate smooth movement from one slide to the next. You can apply the Morph transition to slides to create the appearance of movement in a wide range of things—text, shapes, pictures, SmartArt graphics, and WordArt. Read more here!

PRESENTER COACH: This feature allows you to enter rehearsal mode and, while speaking, receive on-screen guidance about pacing, inclusive language, use of filler words, and culturally insensitive phrases. It even lets you know when you're simply reading off the slide. At the end of each rehearsal session, a detailed report with metrics for additional practice is provided.

> *"Teachers and students should rethink their perception of Power-Point—it's WAY more than a tool for creating slide shows! Students can easily collaborate on whole class projects, create infographics, or even create tutorials with the built in screen recording tool!"*
>
> —Scott Titums (@sdtitmas)

INSTANT SOCIAL MEDIA TEMPLATE

GRADE LEVEL: 3rd-5th

CONTENT AREA(S): History, Reading

COMFORT LEVEL: Medium

LESSON FORMAT: Student Created

QUICK TIP: Students will work more easily with this template if they are familiar with the PowerPoint program, ribbons, and editing features.

DESCRIPTION

Describe a day in history, a famous event, or an important scene from a story, using a social media template.

ISTE STANDARDS

- Educator will provide alternative ways for students to demonstrate competency and reflect on their learning using technology. (7a)
- Educator will explore and apply instructional design principles to create innovative digital learning environments to engage and support learning. (5c)

LESSON SUMMARY

1. This lesson can be done in many different subject areas, but it works best at the end of a unit or as a wrap-up activity.

2. Students choose the event, character, or object they want to portray and use the social media template to illustrate through a photo, username, hashtags, etc.

3. When finished, students can save their slide(s) as jpg files and share using platforms such as Seesaw or Padlet, or they can keep them as a digital file and share on platforms like Flipgrid.

Tons of templates created by teachers for sharing are available for different social media applications. Take a look at educators like Ryan O'Donnel (@creativeedtech), Matt Miller (@Ditchbook), and Tony Vincent (@Tonyvincent) for great ideas to get you started!

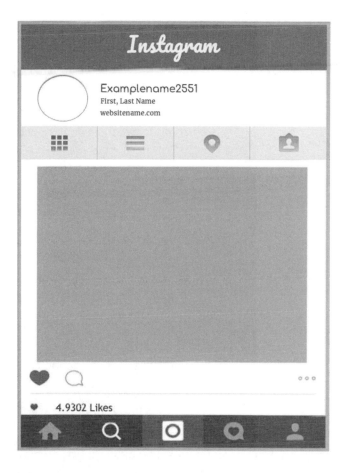

HERE IS A SIMPLE TEMPLATE WE CREATED
TO HELP YOU GET STARTED TODAY!

CLOUD OF COMPLIMENTS

GRADE LEVEL: Any

CONTENT AREA(S): End of Year

COMFORT LEVEL: Medium

LESSON FORMAT: Student Created

QUICK TIP: This activity requires access to Microsoft365, which allows all students to work on the same web-based presentation.

DESCRIPTION

End the year with a fun and encouraging lesson in which students create clouds of compliments over each of their classmates.

ISTE STANDARDS

- Students contribute constructively to project teams, assuming various roles and responsibilities to work effectively toward a common goal. (7c)
- Students create original works or responsibly repurpose or remix digital resources into new creations. (6b)

LESSON SUMMARY

1. Create a presentation containing one slide for every student. Each slide should include a photo of the student. Teachers may upload the photos ahead of time or allow students to take their own photos using the Insert-Picture button.

2. Students work from one slide to the next, writing one kind thing about each of their classmates. By inserting a text box, they can write a descriptive word or leave a fun memory they shared from the year.

3. Students take time to change the font, color, size, and style of their text box so it stands out.

4. As students move through the presentation, each child's slide slowly fills up with compliments.

5. When students are finished, you may wish to "tidy up" some of the slides to ensure that all text is visible and the layout is clean.

6. When all edits are complete, select File, then Export to save the slides as .jpg images. These images can be printed for the students or sent home digitally through applications like Seesaw.

MEMES FOR THEME

DESCRIPTION

Retell the theme of a story by creating fun and amusing meme images! Using PowerPoint, students create a slide including a meme they create through independent image and text selection.

ISTE STANDARDS

- Students choose the appropriate platforms and tools for meeting the desired objectives of their creation or communication. (6a)
- Students create original works or responsibly repurpose or remix digital resources into new creations. (6b)
- Students communicate complex ideas clearly and effectively by creating or using a variety of digital objects such as visualizations, models, or simulations. (6c)

LESSON SUMMARY

1. Start by summarizing the story or topic using one word. Give students a sheet of paper where they can "illustrate" their word and explain in writing why they chose the word.

2. Using their one word as a guide, students create a meme expressing the theme or summary of the book or lesson. Students find copyright-free photos and overlay their text on them.

3. For further explanation, ask students to write a theme statement in the "notes" section on the PowerPoint slide.

GRADE LEVEL: 3rd-5th

CONTENT AREA(S): Reading, Science, History

COMFORT LEVEL: Medium

LESSON FORMAT: Student Created

QUICK TIP: Theme is a standard taught in reading, but this lesson could easily be adapted to summarize a science principle or a historical event.

DIGITAL SCOOT

GRADE LEVEL: Any

CONTENT AREA(S): Any

COMFORT LEVEL: Medium

LESSON FORMAT: Teacher Created

QUICK TIP: Try having one extra device or screen as students rotate to accommodate kids who may work a bit slower or faster than others.

SOCIAL MEDIA

WANT TO CONNECT?
Twitter: @Erintegration
Website: erintegration.com
Instagram: @Erintegration

CHECK OUT ERIN'S RESOURCES, TIPS, AND TRICKS FOR DIGITAL SCOOTS. REMEMBER, YOU CAN TAKE GOOGLE SLIDES AND IMPORT THEM INTO POWERPOINT WITH JUST ONE CLICK!

DESCRIPTION

Imagine taking the old Scoot card game and making it digital! Students load their device with a survey, graph, response question, or activity. Students then "scoot" from device to device and complete the activity displayed on each specific screen.

ISTE STANDARDS

- Educator will design authentic learning activities to align with content area standards and use digital tools and resources to maximize active, deep learning. (5b)

- Educator will explore and apply instructional design principles to create innovative digital learning environments to engage and support learning. (5c)

LESSON SUMMARY

1. This lesson description is to explain how to create a Scoot using Microsoft PowerPoint.

2. Begin by designing a slideshow of activities. Think of each slide as a place for students to respond to a question, create an image or idea, or give their opinion on something.

3. When you are ready to do the activity, share the presentation with all students and ask them each to open it.

4. Tell each student to go to a different slide number so they all have a different activity on their screen.

5. Students complete the task on their screens and then "scoot" to the next device, which has another activity/question to complete.

Digital Scoots keep every student working at once while staying accountable for their own work. Check out on social media the long-time developer and diva of the digital scoot, Erin Flanagan, for scoot ideas for all ages and subject levels!

THE
#INTERACTIVE CLASS @THEMERRILLSEDU
USE THIS SPACE FOR SKETCH NOTES, IDEAS, ETC!

ONENOTE

WHAT IS IT?

OneNote is a digital binder for the twenty-first century to benefit teachers and students. OneNote saves time, promotes digital organization, and makes collaboration easy. Users have an infinite "canvas" on which to add text, ink, audio, video, and pictures. Collaboration can occur on the same page, but also asynchronously anywhere across the notebook. Teachers can add lots of different feedback options—voice, video, ink, text, pictures, stickers, and more. OneNote is also handy for lesson planning, curriculum development, and keeping track of PLC notes.

WHERE CAN I USE IT?

OneNote is available, free of cost, on the web. PC and Mac versions of the program may be downloaded from the Windows and Mac App Store. Mobile users can download the OneNote app from the Android and iOS App Stores.

HOW DOES IT WORK?

OneNote empowers teachers and students to capture information and stay organized. The platform sets the users' creativity free, making creating and sharing lessons easy. The real bonus comes with OneNote's real-time class collaboration, allowing multiple users to work on the same file at once.

Each OneNote Class Notebook is organized into three parts:

- **Student Notebooks:** a private space shared between the teacher and each individual student. Teachers can access every student notebook, but students can only see their own.

- **Content Library:** a read-only space where teachers can share handouts with students.

- **Collaboration Space:** a space where everyone in your class can share, organize, and collaborate.

A OneNote Staff Notebook is set up similarly but is designed for Staff Leaders and Staff members instead of Teachers and Students.

HOW CAN I USE IT IN THE CLASSROOM?

Educators can gather web content and embed existing lessons in their class notebook to create custom lesson plans. Including audio and video recordings will create rich interACTIVE lessons for students. OneNote can also be used as an assessment or progress monitoring tool.

Students can use powerful drawing tools to highlight, annotate slides, sketch diagrams, and take handwritten notes. Teachers can provide a personal workspace for each student, access to a content library for handouts, and a collaboration space for lessons and creative activities.

HIGHLIGHTED FEATURES

ONENOTE "CANVAS": A key part of OneNote is the flexible "canvas" that allows you to use it like digital paper. Multimedia such as text, pictures, audio, video, and ink are all compatible. After inserting the media, you can arrange it however you see fit.

INSERT AUDIO: Users can insert audio anywhere on the page. Students can record themselves reading, or educators can provide richer feedback.

IMMERSIVE READER: Microsoft's Immersive Reader is a full-screen reading experience to increase readability of content in applications. This tool is designed to support students with dyslexia and dysgraphia in the classroom, but it can support anyone who wants to make reading on their device easier.

EMBED APPS INTO ONENOTE: App smashing is simple in OneNote! Users can paste URLs to other apps to interactively embed into OneNote. Some of the compatible apps include YouTube, Flipgrid, Buncee, Geogebra, Quizlet, Sway, Forms, Vimeo, and EdPuzzle.

DICTATION: Users can use the built-in text-to-speech feature for inclusive writing.

DIGITAL INK: OneNote on Windows, 365 Online, and iPad all support digital inking.

MATH SUPPORT: Many versions of OneNote support math, including ink to math, helping solve math equations, and immersive reader to support students with math difficulties.

TO SEE WHICH FEATURES ARE COMPATIBLE WITH YOUR DEVICE, SCAN THE QR CODE.

EXPLORE HERE FOR ALL THINGS ONENOTE EDU.

RUNNING RECORDS

GRADE LEVEL: Any

CONTENT AREA(S): Reading

COMFORT LEVEL: Beginner

LESSON FORMAT: Teacher Created

QUICK TIP: Add an audio recording of each student at the beginning of the year, and then again throughout the year to hear the progress they've made.

DESCRIPTION

Lose the paper and add new capabilities to your running records binder! With this simple template, you can keep track of all of your students' reading progress and even add audio recordings of them!

ISTE STANDARDS

- Educator will use technology to design and implement a variety of formative and summative assessments to accommodate learner needs, provide timely feedback to students, and inform instruction. (7b)

- Educator will use assessment data to guide progress and communicate with students, parents, and education stakeholders to build student self-direction. (7c)

LESSON SUMMARY

1. Create a new notebook in OneNote.

2. Rename the sections, creating one for each student in your class.

3. After you have finished setting up your notebook, tap or click on the student section of your choice.

4. Tap or click on "insert" and then tap on the image. Upload the template from your saved files.

5. You can resize the image by clicking on it and pulling the corners out.

6. When a student is ready to read, tap on "draw." This allows you to annotate over the template. We recommend writing the date on the top title line.

7. If you would like to record the student, tap or click on "insert" and then "audio recording."

8. As your student reads, annotate over the template as needed.

9. If you are recording your student's audio, tap or click "stop" to turn off the recording. You can move the audio recording box anywhere on the screen, placing it out of the way of the template.

| Date:

Title:

Level: | Accuracy

correct = # of words

_____

Accuracy %

_____ % | Comprehension

Characters yes / no

Setting yes / no

Plot yes / no

Main Idea yes / no | Comprehension Rubric Score (/24)

_____ | Fluency

Fluency Rubric Score (/16)

_____ | Level

Easy Instructional

Hard

100-95%

95-90%

Below 90% |
|---|---|---|---|---|---|

GET STARTED NOW! DOWNLOAD THE TEMPLATE TO GET YOUR RUNNING RECORDS DIGITAL AND MORE ACCESSIBLE.

"I have fallen in love with OneNote! I have been searching for an easy way to take my run-of-the-mill interactive notebooks in class and make them digital, and OneNote is the answer! I love that I can share certain components with students, I can assign questions or writing prompts, and it's a one-stop shop."

—Andy Knueven (@MRCoachK15)

PIRATE MAP

GRADE LEVEL: 3rd-5th

CONTENT AREA(S): History, Science, Reading

COMFORT LEVEL: Medium

LESSON FORMAT: Teacher Created

QUICK TIP: This lesson can be created in many subject areas, but it works well with a topic or unit in which discovery and research are involved.

DESCRIPTION

Use the infinite canvas feature in OneNote to create a lesson in which students can "explore" the content like pirates: each assignment is where X marks the spot!

ISTE STANDARDS

- The educator will establish a learning culture to promote curiosity and critical examination of online resources and foster digital literacy and media fluency. (3b)
- Educator will explore and apply instructional design principles to create innovative digital learning environments to engage and support learning. (5c)

LESSON SUMMARY

1. Create the first lesson activity in the top left corner of the OneNote workspace. This will make it easy for students to find the place to start working.

2. After the first activity, simply use the line and arrow tool to create the "pirate map" drawing effect. Use a .jpg image or a doodle of your own for the "X" to mark the next activity spot.

3. Have fun spreading out the activities. Students will enjoy searching for the "X" and seeing where the next activity is. An open space is also good to have in case students are going to be typing, inking, or doing anything requiring some space on the canvas.

4. Make the activities interesting. Try adding audio, integrating links, videoing responses (Flipgrid is great for this!), or including online web hunts, creative writing, or anything else you have available to pull resources from.

5. When finished, distribute the OneNote assignment by going to the Classroom Notebook tab, then the "distribute" page, and click either "individual" or "group" distribution.

Integrate articles and apps using web links!

"To Do boxes" are an easy way to help students keep track of the work they've completed.

☐ Read through Growing Up In Slavery and when finished, share your thoughts on Flipgrid!

In Fannie's Shoes

Now imagine yourself in Fannie's shoes when she was a child.

- What are some of the hardest things about being a slave?
- Describe your family. What do they do? What do you respect about them?
- Describe the plantation where you live. How is your house different from your master's?

☐ Imagine it is 1860. You are one of 4 million slaves in the United States. Follow along in the journey as you start...

1. On the plantation
2. Then as you escape
3. You hopefully will reach safety
4. And end up achieving freedom

Begin your journey!

Harriet Tubman: Leading the Way to Freedom

Create spaces where students can respond and share.

Learn more about Harriet Tubman using the resources below.

Write a Secret Letter

You are a secret agent on the Underground Railroad writing to a stationmaster in Philadelphia. Can you drag the words and phrases to complete the letter?
Give it a try!

When you're done, try writing your own letter!

Begin your letter here...

Add in the text boxes ahead of time to make typing and formatting easier for students!

Question	Source	Answer
Describe Harriet Tubman's childhood. What was one of her jobs as a child? How did she get a scar on her head?	Library of Congress	
Describe Harriet Tubman's escape from slavery. When did she flee? Where did she go? What made her go back?	Biography article	
What were some of the reasons that Harriet Tubman's rescues were so successful? How did she discourage slaves who wanted to turn back?	PBS Website	
How did Harriet Tubman help the Union during the Civil War?	National Geographic	
After the Civil War, how did Harriet Tubman continue to fight for justice and help those in need?	National Women's Hall of Fame	

Tip: If you have a more time-consuming activity or one giving more free choice, such as a web hunt or interactive website, consider making it the last activity. This allows students to complete the other parts of the map rather than getting stuck exploring just one.

ONEDERFUL SUB PLANS

GRADE LEVEL: 3rd-5th

CONTENT AREA(S): Any

COMFORT LEVEL: Medium

LESSON FORMAT: Teacher Created

QUICK TIP: Try assigning similar lessons during independent work time, so when it's time for students to work in OneNote without you, they will know how to troubleshoot and work efficiently.

DESCRIPTION

Not every activity or lesson left for students to do with a substitute can be done independently, but using OneNote gives you the freedom to leave unit-like, multimedia assignments for students to work on and learn from while you're out.

ISTE STANDARDS

- Educator will use technology to create, adapt, and personalize learning experiences to foster independent learning and accommodate learner differences and needs. (5a)

- Educator will use technology to design and implement a variety of formative and summative assessments to accommodate learner needs, provide timely feedback to students, and inform instruction. (7b)

LESSON SUMMARY

1. Create a new OneNote document and name it for the day you are going to be out (e.g., Reading, Tuesday the 12th).

2. Using the array of features available in OneNote, create lessons for students to complete based on the current subject and unit of study. These are some of our favorite features for creating sub plans:

   - Create text boxes with directions. Then add audio beside them, giving students the option to listen through the steps.

   - After each activity, create To Do boxes that students can check off when they have completed the assignment.

   - Microsoft Forms easily embed into OneNote. Try creating a form with a video or article as part of it, or some short answer responses or a rank or order question.

   - Flipgrid now integrates into OneNote seamlessly, so try adding some video response components to the lessons. Flipgrid allows attachments and has amazing partnerships with sites such as Wonderopolis, Rise and Grind, and

ThingLink's, which always add extra depth and engagement to a lesson.

- You can always just add simple links for students to interact with along with Microsoft Word Documents and so much more!

3. When finished, distribute the OneNote assignment by going to the Classroom Notebook tab and clicking "distribute page" and then "group distribution."

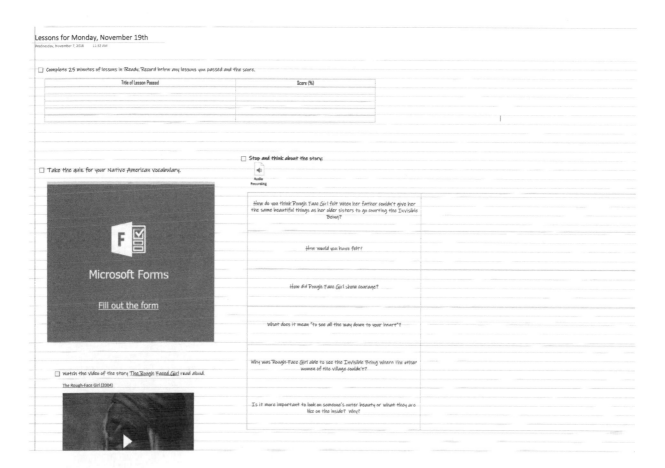

THINGLINK

WHAT IS IT?

ThingLink's uses the creation of digital media to engage students of different ages and learning styles. It develops collaboration and communication skills while engaging in real-world learning experiences. ThingLink's supports digital literacy, research, and documentation of learning through the art of storytelling.

WHERE CAN I USE IT?

ThingLink's works with existing technology, including tablets, smartphones, and desktops. Teachers can set up an account for free without the classroom management option. Single teacher subscriptions including the classroom management feature start at $35 a year for image, video, and 360° editors.

HOW DOES IT WORK?

ThingLink's creates a digital workspace where you can tag images, videos, and 360° media with in-stant access to additional information, audio, video, embedded material, and web links. ThingLink's supports digital literacy, research, and documentation of learning while providing students with an engaging platform for sharing their learning and creativity.

HOW CAN I USE IT IN THE CLASSROOM?

You can empower students as content creators and develop digital literacy and storytelling skills both inside and outside the classroom. Easily create engaging learning materials and virtual tours with your students on any topic in your own language. Allow students to create their own presentations based on their learning in the classroom. Take a class photo and link to it student work from every child for a parent presentation, walk through a historical painting or document, or give a virtual tour of your new classroom for the year.

HIGHLIGHTED FEATURES

INTERACTIVE 360° VIDEO: ThingLink's growing collection of 360° stories lets learners of any country and age experience places and phenomena with the help of a virtual learning assistant. For creation, students can use ThingLink's 360° image editor to easily make virtual tours or 360° documentaries with audio narration, images, videos, and quizzes, engaging students like never before.

CUSTOM CONTENT AND LAYOUTS: Save time and make professional-looking visuals by customizing designs for tags and icons, or simply embed any third-party content.

MOBILE APP: ThingLink's mobile app is the easiest way to save and share notes and observations about real-world spaces, situations, and artifacts. It is ideal for classroom and workplace learning, with direct voice recording to camera photos!

CLOUD LEARNING: Cloud learning is the easiest and most cost-efficient way to build real-world learning experiences without logistical hassle. It is suitable for online lectures, technical and vocational education, workplace learning, campus tours, and virtual field trips.

ThingLink now has Immersive Reader integrated, which makes a powerful combination for any inclusive classroom! It creates an accessible reading experience that has been proven to improve reading comprehension for learners.

WANT TO CONNECT?
Twitter: @ThingLink's
Website: thinglink.com
Instagram: @ThingLink's

SOCIAL MEDIA

YEARBOOK MEMORY WALL

GRADE LEVEL: Any

CONTENT AREA(S): Any

COMFORT LEVEL: Beginner

LESSON FORMAT: Teacher or Student Created

QUICK TIP: If you don't want to wait for the class picture or student shots to be taken for the yearbook, take your own!

DESCRIPTION

Use the class photo as a starting point to pin student work all together in one place. Create a class showcase of work to be shared during open house, STEAM night, or through a weekly parent email update.

ISTE STANDARDS

- Educator will use collaborative tools to expand students' authentic, real-world learning experiences by engaging virtually with experts, teams, and students—locally and globally. (4c)

- Educator will foster a culture where students take ownership of their learning goals and outcomes in both independent and group settings. (6a)

- Educator will provide alternative ways for students to demonstrate competency and reflect on their learning using technology. (7a)

LESSON SUMMARY

1. Start with a class group picture or a page of individual student photos representing each student.

2. Based on teacher direction, students each pin their spot in the photo and upload their individual student artifact. These could be photos of work, or web links connecting student work from applications such as Flipgrid, Buncee, Adobe, or Book Creator.

3. Once all student work has been added, share the finished ThingLink's at school through a QR code, with parents through a link to a platform like Seesaw, or simply through an email.

PRESIDENT'S RESEARCH

DESCRIPTION

Create an InterACTIVE poster in which your students collaboratively become the authors. Easily generate a classroom discussion, using ThingLink's's hotspots to efficiently open projects.

ISTE STANDARDS

- Students understand the fundamental concepts of technology operations, demonstrate the ability to choose, use, and troubleshoot current technologies, and are able to transfer their knowledge to explore emerging technologies. (1d)

- Students plan and employ effective research strategies to locate information and other resources for their intellectual or creative pursuits. (3a)

- Students evaluate the accuracy, perspective, credibility, and relevance of information, media, data, or other resources. (3b)

- Students curate information from digital resources, using a variety of tools and methods to create collections of artifacts to demonstrate meaningful connections or conclusions. (3c)

GRADE LEVEL: Any

CONTENT AREA(S): Social Studies or Writing

COMFORT LEVEL: Medium

LESSON FORMAT: Student and Teacher Created

QUICK TIP: Try the embedded Microsoft Immersive Reader when doing this project with kindergarten through 2nd grade students or with English Language Learner students.

LESSON SUMMARY

1. Assign each student or group a president. Ask them to conduct the proper research and record the necessary facts to fit your standards.
2. Ask the students to complete a writing task, using the research they have studied.
3. After completing the writing, have the students or groups pull out highlighted facts (the things they didn't know about each president or other interesting information), and give them time to compose a brief summarization of their study.
4. Using an app like Flipgrid, Buncee, or Seesaw, ask the students to create a video of their summary. *Hint:* Students could #AppSmash from ChatterPix into Flipgrid, where they would animate their president's mouth.
5. Have a digital poster of all the presidents' pictures ready. Upload this file into ThingLink's.
6. When ready to submit the students' final response, copy the share code from the selected app and paste it into ThingLink's.
7. ThingLink's will automatically generate a hotspot so others can click the area to open files.

TRY APP SMASHING! After you have collected all responses, share the ThingLink's URL on Seesaw for parents to view!

TOUR MY CLASSROOM

GRADE LEVEL: Any

CONTENT AREA(S): Start of the year

COMFORT LEVEL: Beginner

LESSON FORMAT: Teacher Created

QUICK TIP: This would be a fun and interactive way to engage new students and their families when you meet before school starts.

DESCRIPTION

Help students easily maneuver their way around your classroom. No more interrupted moments or questions about where to find things. This activity will help your students find the answers they are looking for.

ISTE STANDARDS

- Educator will model and nurture creativity and creative expression to communicate ideas, knowledge, or connections. (6d)
- Educator will foster a culture where students take ownership of their learning goals and outcomes in both independent and group settings. (6a)

LESSON SUMMARY

1. Take a picture of your classroom.
2. Upload the image to ThingLink's.
3. Locate the important areas in your photo, and then add the hot spots (or places of interest) for the students to tap or click on.
4. Enter the necessary information on your hot spots, using videos and other media.
5. Share the link on Seesaw, Microsoft's Teams, or Google Classroom. This will allow students to have the ability to go back and revisit the file if needed. It also keeps your parents informed!

THE #INTERACTIVE CLASS @THEMERRILLSEDU

USE THIS SPACE FOR SKETCH NOTES, IDEAS, ETC!

APPLE CLIPS

WHAT IS IT?

Clips is an iOS app you can use for making and sharing fun videos with text, effects, graphics, and more. Videos can be put together through short "clips" that can be rearranged, filtered, closed captioned, and even set to music. The platform is user friendly and easily learned by students of all ages.

WHERE CAN I USE IT?

Apple Clips is free and available in the Apple Store for both iPhone and iPad.

HOW DOES IT WORK?

Getting started is simple and easy. Just hold the record button to capture video on the spot, or grab a video clip or photo from your library. You can pinch and drag while recording to smoothly zoom and pan across images for extra features. Once videos are recorded, you can edit them by clipping them down, or you can rearrange them by simply holding and dragging. You have the ability to voice over video and take out either original audio or recorded audio, which gives you many editing options.

HOW CAN I USE IT IN THE CLASSROOM?

Inspire your students to tell stories with engaging visuals. Students can record live titles to caption their videos—even in other languages—and apply stickers, labels, and posters to illustrate videos from science projects to math problems. Students can also use photos and videos from their library or record themselves as part of their video. Clips can be used to create story summaries, math explanations, book reviews, research projects, movie trailers, school announcements, weekly classroom highlight videos, and much more!

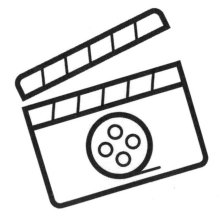

HIGHLIGHTED FEATURES

LIVE TITLES: Live Titles lets you easily create animated captions and titles just by talking. Simply speak while recording, and text automatically appears onscreen, synced with your voice. Tap the clip to easily edit text, add punctuation, or change the style of your title.

PERSONALIZATION: Instantly add your personal touches to videos by applying 3D stickers, adding animated emojis, or recording through the retro camcorder feature.

SELFIE SCENES: Selfie Scenes use the TrueDepth camera to place you in beautifully animated landscapes, a mad scientist's lab, and even the opening action scene from Disney Pixar's Incredibles 2. Each scene is a full 360° experience, so the scene surrounds you on all sides regardless of how you move your device.

ICLOUD SYNC: Clips works with iCloud, so you can view and edit any of your projects on all your devices. Capture a moment on iPhone, then use iPad to continue creating.

FULL SCREEN POSTERS: Clips has many full-screen posters featuring colorfully animated or stop-motion backgrounds available to mix in as part of your video.

MUSIC: You can choose from dozens of music tracks included in Clips, able to intelligently adjust to match the length of your video, or you can import personally created music straight from Garage Band.

TRAPPED IN A VIDEO GAME

GRADE LEVEL: Any

CONTENT AREA(S): Math (but could be adapted for any subject)

COMFORT LEVEL: Beginner

LESSON FORMAT: Teacher Created

QUICK TIP: *This feature only works with iPhone X or higher. If you don't have a recently purchased device, try using the filters (located by tapping the rainbow star) instead of "scenes."

DESCRIPTION

How would your students react if their teacher was stuck in a video game? Oh, no! Easily "trap" yourself in a video game using Apple Clips' AR "Scenes."

ISTE STANDARDS

- Educator will design authentic learning activities to align with content area standards and use digital tools and resources to maximize active, deep learning. (5b)

- Educator will explore and apply instructional design principles to create innovative digital learning environments to engage and support learning. (5c)

LESSON SUMMARY

1. Open Apple Clips and tap on "scenes" (iPhone X or higher*).

2. Scroll through the selections and choose "8 Bit." Tap "select." This will place you in an augmented reality video game scene. You can move the device around to change the background, because it is a 360° image.

3. Now you're ready to record your first challenge. Either hold down or swipe up on the red "record" button to begin recording. Give your students the challenge.

4. Tap the "sharrow" (or "export") icon, and tap "save video." The video is now saved to your camera roll. Repeat as necessary.

TRY APP SMASHING! Take your video and #AppSmash it into programs like Flipgrid, where you can create multiple "levels" for students to complete or break out of!

 Tips and Tricks: To "free" yourself from the video game, practice trimming the "8 Bit" clip into a clip recorded without a filter.

Record multiple challenges and submit the challenges as a student on Flipgrid. Have the students respond directly to you, which will create an organized thread.

Don't have an iPhone X or higher? Use the different sketch filters (located by tapping the "rainbow star" icon) to create the effect of being drawn into a storybook.

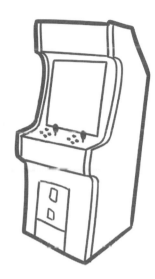

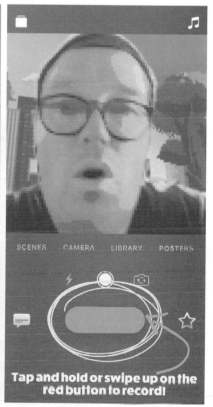

STORY SKETCHES

GRADE LEVEL: 2nd-5th

CONTENT AREA(S): Reading

COMFORT LEVEL: Medium

LESSON FORMAT: Student Created

QUICK TIP: Teachers can create a fun video to launch a lesson or introduce a new story or standard.

DESCRIPTION

Jump into a story and create videos from "inside" the story. Instantly become a story sketch as you communicate your thoughts and ideas as a drawing.

ISTE STANDARDS

- Students publish or present content to customize the message and medium for their intended audiences. (6d)

LESSON SUMMARY

1. Begin by reviewing the specific reading standard with the class. For example, the standard might be on inferring a character's thoughts and emotions.

2. Once the standard has been reviewed, students create several video clips, using one of the many sketch filters to record their answers.

3. The filter will make it appear as if they were dropped into the story book as part of the illustrations.

4. To increase the depth of the lesson, students could film several sketched videos and clip them together. They could possibly answer several questions throughout the clips or respond to a change in time throughout the story (e.g., plot, character's actions or emotions, etc.).

5. When finished, students save their clip(s) and download to the device. From there they can share with the class on the platform of the teacher's choice.

TRY APP SMASHING! Try "sketching" yourself into a story, and then #AppSmash the video into other creation platforms such as Book Creator, Flipgrid, or Adobe Spark.

CHOICES IN SCENES

Sketchbook Scene

CHOICES IN FILTERS

Comic book

Comic mono

Ink

Watercolor

Watercolor mono

EMOJI STORY SUMMARY

GRADE LEVEL: 3rd-5th

CONTENT AREA(S): Reading

COMFORT LEVEL: Beginner

LESSON FORMAT: Student Created

QUICK TIP: Preloading emoji images onto student devices makes this activity easier for younger students.

DESCRIPTION

Try this spinoff of the old story summary, in which students come up with a synopsis of a story and represent it with emojis. Students can add music and voice recording over for the final summary video.

ISTE STANDARDS

- Students create original works or responsibly repurpose or remix digital resources into new creations. (6b)

- Students communicate complex ideas clearly and effectively by creating or using a variety of digital objects such as visualizations, models, or simulations. (6c)

- Students publish or present content to customize the message and medium for their intended audiences. (6d)

LESSON SUMMARY

1. Just as with any summary, students begin by retelling the story in their own words. This includes characters, main events, and possibly an ending theme or moral to the story. The summary depth and length should reflect the age and grade of the students.

2. After forming their summary—whether written or not—students begin matching various people, events, etc., with different emojis.

3. Emojis can be preselected by the teacher, or students can search for images simply using "emoji _____" as key words. As students find images, they should save them to their devices.

4. Once emojis have been chosen and ordered, students open a new project and choose the first emoji photo from the library.

5. To record, simply hold down the record button for the length of time it takes them to speak over and read the part of the summary correlating to the specific emoji.

6. Students keep repeating and adding all the emojis needed for their summary.

LESSON EXAMPLE:

STORY: Three Little Pigs

SUMMARY: The three little pigs set out to build houses to keep them safe from the big, bad wolf. The first two houses are made of straw and sticks, and the wolf is able to easily blow them down. The third house, made of bricks, keeps the pigs safe.

EMOJIS:

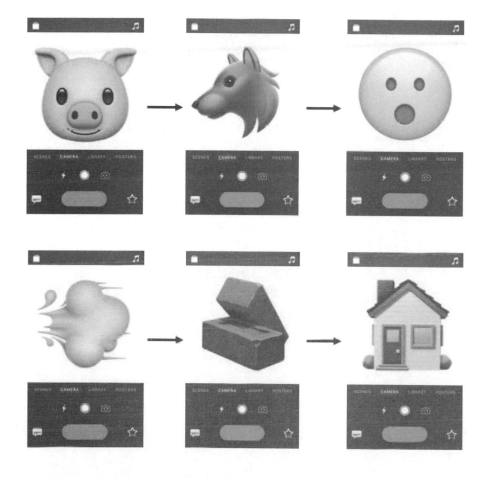

STUDENT SCAVENGER HUNT

GRADE LEVEL: Any

CONTENT AREA(S): All

COMFORT LEVEL: Beginner

LESSON FORMAT: Student Created

QUICK TIP: Model how students can use stickers, titles, and emojis to make the video more appealing!

DESCRIPTION

Give students a chance to demonstrate mastery by showing what they know through gamified hunts both inside and outside of the classroom. Students keep a list of clips to document all they find on their hunt.

ISTE STANDARDS

- Students know and use a deliberate design process for generating ideas, testing theories, creating innovative artifacts, or solving authentic problems. (4a)

- Students contribute constructively to project teams, assuming various roles and responsibilities to work effectively toward a common goal. (7c)

- Students curate information from digital resources, using a variety of tools and methods to create collections of artifacts to demonstrate meaningful connections or conclusions. (3c)

LESSON SUMMARY

1. Assign a scavenger hunt task to your students.

2. Have the students use Apple Clips to capture what they find. Encourage them to highlight important information with stickers or titles.

3. Allow the students to go back and preview the clips. Edit, trim, or delete as needed.

4. Share the video with the class to generate a group discussion.

TRY APP SMASHING! Take your video and #AppSmash it into programs like Flipgrid for a creative classroom discussion. You can also #AppSmash it into Seesaw to share with families!

ADDITIONAL LESSON IDEAS

Students could go hunting for...

- 2D and 3D shapes

- Lines and angles

- Living and nonliving things

- ABC words starting with...

- Text features

- Seeds, flowers, and plant features

- Things of various colors (possibly in rainbow order)

- Items of a certain length ("this many" inches or feet long)

"Start small and don't be afraid to provide your students 'tinker' time. A lot of times, students can troubleshoot the technology faster than we can!"
—Karie Frauenhoffer (@legitkfrauey)

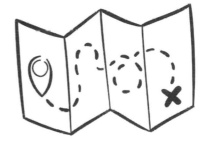

#OURDAYINAMINUTE

GRADE LEVEL: Any

CONTENT AREA(S): All

COMFORT LEVEL: Beginner

LESSON FORMAT: Teacher Created

QUICK TIP: This works wonderfully if your district blocks Instagram. Remember, try to keep the video under 1 minute for higher viewer engagement.

DESCRIPTION

Turn your classroom walls into windows! Keep your parents in the loop about the things happening in class. Use Apple Clips to take short, quick shots throughout the day and easily create a compilation highlighting the happenings!

ISTE STANDARDS

- Educator will shape, advance, and accelerate a shared vision for empowered learning with technology by engaging with education stakeholders. (2a)

- Educator will demonstrate cultural competency when communicating with students, parents, and colleagues and interact with them as co-collaborators in student learning. (4d)

LESSON SUMMARY

1. Open Apple Clips and tap on "Posters." Select a poster of your choice and tap the text to edit it. This will be the first thing to appear in your video.

2. Periodically, open Apple Clips. As you're monitoring your students, record short clips of what is happening in your classroom. These should be two to four seconds long—not long shots.

3. After the day is over, tap on the "music note" icon (top right). Select a background song fitting your day. Note: these songs will intelligently start and stop according to your clips, so you do not need to edit the music.

4. Preview your video, deleting any unnecessary shots. Tap on the "sharrow" (or "export") icon. Tap "save video" to save it to your iPhone's camera roll.

5. Share the video with parents in an email or your preferred method of communication.

TRY APP SMASHING! Take your video and #AppSmash it into programs like Seesaw for parent involvement.

THE #INTERACTIVE CLASS @THEMERRILLSEDU

USE THIS SPACE FOR SKETCH NOTES, IDEAS, ETC!

BOOK CREATOR

WHAT IS IT?

Book Creator is a simple tool for creating digital books. Create your own teaching resources or have your students take the reins. Students can combine text, images, audio, and video to create the perfect book for any occasion.

WHERE CAN I USE IT?

Download the Book Creator app for iPad. It is free for one book or $4.99 for the full version. It's also available for Chromebooks at $60 per year for 180 books (3 libraries, 60 books in each library), with support for real-time collaboration.

HOW DOES IT WORK?

It doesn't matter what subject or grade level you're teaching—students can demonstrate their understanding by creating a book. Writing a book is a fantastic way to make connections in learning. Students create a finished product, giving them a platform for sharing their learning with peers or others.

To get started, simply choose the shape and size of the book, customize colors, and add a title with text. You can also add images to the front page before adding a new page. There you will have a double spread of blank pages, ready to be designed.

HOW CAN I USE IT IN THE CLASSROOM?

Book Creator provides ways for students to publish work to an authentic audience. Students are able to demonstrate understanding and utilize their creativity. It also motivates reluctant writers. Combine text, images, audio, and video to create interACTIVE stories, digital portfolios, research journals, poetry books, science reports, and much more.

GET STARTED NOW! LEARN MORE #APPSMASHING WITH BOOK CREATOR HERE!

BOOK CREATOR & FLIPGRID
INTEGRATE AND CREATE!
BY: @MRMERRILLSCLASS

HIGHLIGHTED FEATURES

AUTODRAW: Now you can use AI to turn clumsy doodles into doodled art. Originally created by Google's Creative Lab, AutoDraw identifies what you are attempting to draw, and then transforms it into a work of art.

MAGIC INK: Use unique colors to make your illustrations stand out. You can even use Magic Ink as a highlighter!

PEN TOOL: Use the pen tool to draw and annotate your book vand add shapes and lines.

EMOJIS: Add emojis and easily move them around your book for added fun.

FILL TOOL: Quickly fill in your shapes or drawing with this paint bucket tool.

50+ FONTS: Book Creator offers more than fifty hand-picked fonts for you to choose from.

PHOTOS AND IMAGES: Add photos and images from your device's photo library, from the web, or use the iPad's camera.

MULTIMEDIA: Add video and music, and even record your voice.

SNAP TO GRID: Resize, rotate, and position content as you like with guidelines and snap positioning.

MULTIPLE LAYOUTS: Choose from portrait, landscape, or square book sizes. There are even comic book templates!

READ IN IBOOKS: With a quick tap, you're able to export your book to iBooks!

SHARING: Send your book via email, AirDrop to iPhone, iPad, or Mac, upload to a cloud based service, export as a PDF, or publish to the eBooks Store.

 GET STARTED NOW! CHECK OUT THE AMAZING EBOOKS, CREATED BY THE BOOK CREATOR STAFF, FOR MORE LESSON IDEAS AND TUTORIALS.

WANT TO CONNECT?
Twitter: @BookCreatorApp
Website: bookcreator.com
Instagram: @BookCreatorApp

INTERACTIVE WORD WALL BOOK

GRADE LEVEL: K-2nd

CONTENT AREA(S): Reading or Writing

COMFORT LEVEL: Beginner

LESSON FORMAT: Student Created

QUICK TIP: Teach your students to keep their "word wall" words in alphabetical order.

DESCRIPTION

Do your students constantly ask you how to spell words? Help your students with spelling and writing with this interACTIVE word wall book!

ISTE STANDARDS

- Students create original works or responsibly repurpose or remix digital resources into new creations. (6b)

LESSON SUMMARY

1. Open the Book Creator app or website and create a new book. You can select from several different sizes.

2. Be sure to leave the first page (the cover page) blank. We like to let the students decorate the first page so they know exactly what the book looks like.

3. On the second page, add a text box and type the letter "A." Move the "A" to the top of the page.

4. Next, ask students to duplicate the page, and then edit the "A" to a "B." Repeat this process for all the letters.

5. When ready, ask students to add words to the appropriate pages. Make sure the students have the words spelled correctly.

6. Ask students to record an audio recording of each word, so they can play the recording as needed.

FIVE SENSES EBOOK

DESCRIPTION

Put a spin on learning about the five senses! Ask your students to describe their senses in detail by adding multimedia to create an eBook.

ISTE STANDARDS

- Students build knowledge by actively exploring real-world issues and problems, developing ideas and theories, and pursuing answers and solutions. (3d)
- Students communicate complex ideas clearly and effectively by creating or using a variety of digital objects such as visualizations, models, or simulations. (6c)
- Students publish or present content to customize the message and medium for their intended audiences. (6d)

LESSON SUMMARY

1. Give your students a specific amount of time to photograph or video different ways of using the Five Senses. This could be done outside, too.

2. When time is up, have the students open Book Creator. Remember, students should not add anything to the cover page. They should start on Page Two.

3. On Page Two, ask the students to add their first sense. They can add text and multimedia.

4. Tap or click on the "+" button to the right to add a new page.

5. Repeat the process above for each sense.

6. When all senses have been completed, allow the students to go back and edit the cover page. Remind them to add their own names.

7. If you have students who finish early, you can ask them to go back and add an audio recording of themselves reading the page. This adds a level of accessibility to the project.

8. When completed, export the eBook as a PDF or eBook file to save.

GRADE LEVEL: K-2nd

CONTENT AREA(S): Science or Reading

COMFORT LEVEL: Beginner

LESSON FORMAT: Student Created

QUICK TIP: Give the students a maximum number of photographs for each category. This way they can focus on writing.

TRY APP SMASHING!

Once completed, share the Book Creator project on Seesaw for parents to view!

CLASS NARRATIVE

GRADE LEVEL: Any

CONTENT AREA(S): Writing

COMFORT LEVEL: Beginner

LESSON FORMAT: Student Created

QUICK TIP: You'll need the paid version of Book Creator Chrome for this lesson.

DESCRIPTION

Easily share student writing with the class, school, and parents through the creation of class narratives!

ISTE STANDARDS

- Students create original works or responsibly repurpose or remix digital resources into new creations. (6b)
- Students publish or present content that customizes the message and medium for their intended audiences. (6d)
- Students contribute constructively to project teams, assuming various roles and responsibilities to work effectively toward a common goal. (7c)

LESSON SUMMARY

1. Using the paid version of Book Creator for Chrome, start a new book.

2. Click the "social sharing" icon and click "Start Collaboration." Click on "Show invite code for others to join." This will generate a code for you to share with all students. Display this code on the board.

3. Assign page numbers to each student, so they understand the space they have to work with.

4. On the assigned page, ask students to type their narrative writing. Encourage students to use multimedia, read their writing aloud, or take a picture of their published writing to include on the page.

5. When the class is finished, you will have curated all student writing in one place.

TRY APP SMASHING! Once completed, share the final Book Creator project on Seesaw. Be sure to tag all families so everyone has access!

YEAR-END MEMORY BOOKS

DESCRIPTION

Send your students off at the end of the school year with something they can download and save forever! Year-end memory books are a collaborative way to capture a year's worth of fun.

ISTE STANDARDS

- Students create original works or responsibly repurpose or remix digital resources into new creations. (6b)
- Students contribute constructively to project teams, assuming various roles and responsibilities to work effectively toward a common goal. (7c)

GRADE LEVEL: Any

CONTENT AREA(S):
Writing/Reading

COMFORT LEVEL: Beginner

LESSON FORMAT: Student Created

QUICK TIP: Visit your social media account to remember all of the incredible things the class did throughout the year. The students will love looking back, and this way nothing gets missed!

LESSON SUMMARY

1. Open Book Creator and turn on the "collaboration" feature so students can work together in the same book.
2. As a whole group, discuss various activities the class has completed throughout the year.
3. Give each student a Post-It note and explain they are to put their name and top three memories on the note.
4. Open a Word or Google doc and start a table with all student names on the left side, leaving the right side blank.
5. Call students up one by one and give them their first choice of memory. If someone else has already selected it, move on to the student's second (or third) choice.
6. Once all students are accounted for, display the final list on the board.
7. Ask students to write about why they liked the memory they selected.
8. When ready, ask the students to type their writing into the Book Creator book you created. Be sure you start on Page Two, and not on the Cover Page. (You can ask students to design the cover page at any time.)
9. Tap or click on the "+" button to the right to add a new page.
10. Once the writing is done, ask the students to decorate their page by changing the background and adding multimedia.
11. Select a student (or students) to design a cover
12. When all student work is completed, export the eBook as a PDF or eBook file to save.

STAFF INTRODUCTION BOOK

GRADE LEVEL: Any

CONTENT AREA(S): Beginning of School

COMFORT LEVEL: Beginner

LESSON FORMAT: Staff Created

QUICK TIP: Work on this before school gets out for the summer and send the finished book of introductions to families before the first day of school next fall.

DESCRIPTION

Create a school-wide book as a fun way to introduce the staff to new and returning students and welcome them back to the building in the fall.

ISTE STANDARDS

- Educator will demonstrate cultural competency when communicating with students, parents, and colleagues, and interact with them as co-collaborators in student learning. (4d)

- Educators will model and nurture creativity and creative expression to communicate ideas, knowledge, or connections. (6d)

LESSON SUMMARY

1. Have one staff member—possibly the librarian, reading coach, or person who works with school outreach—create a new book.

2. Turn on the "collaboration" mode so multiple people can work at one time.

3. For easy organization and less confusion when designing, assign teacher names at the top of each page prior to sharing with staff.

4. Share the invite code with staff members so they can decorate their page as they see fit. Teachers, administrators, and staff can add photos, videos, Google Form questionnaires, Google Slide decks, and even record their own voice messages.

5. When the book is complete, save and send to parents before school starting.

USE THIS SPACE FOR SKETCH NOTES, IDEAS, ETC!

PICCOLLAGE EDU

WHAT IS IT?

PicCollage EDU is a safe and user-friendly collage app. With no account required to use the app and no social sharing features, it's perfect for young children and for classroom use. Easily create amazing collages with PicCollage EDU and save them to your device or print them out!

WHERE CAN I USE IT?

PicCollage EDU is available for iOS for $1.99. PicCollage is available for iOS, Android, and Windows for free, but it does not have security features enabled. If you choose to use PicCollage over PicCollageEDU, please be aware of the security differences between the two apps.

HOW DOES IT WORK?

Students pick a template or design their own freestyle collage. PicCollage EDU also offers hundreds of free backgrounds, fun stickers, and fonts. Then students are able to add multimedia (drawings, safe search web images [PicCollage EDU only], stickers, and animations) to create their digital image.

HOW CAN I USE IT IN THE CLASSROOM?

Students can use templates or freestyle collages to design visual thinking models to share vocabulary terms, math strategies, science-related topics, and more. These collages can be added into other programs such as Seesaw, Book Creator, Flipgrid, Google Slides, OneNote, and many others.

HIGHLIGHTED FEATURES

SAFE WEB SEARCH: PicCollage EDU provides a safe web search when students are looking for images to use in their collages. Note: this feature is unavailable on PicCollage.

IMPORT PHOTOS: Students can easily import photos from the camera roll to use in their collages.

ROTATE, RESIZE: With a few gestures, students can rotate and resize their collage. They're also able to delete unwanted scraps.

CLIP PHOTOS: To clip a photo, outline the area you wish to use. Then cut and paste as needed.

DOODLES: Use the "Doodle" tool to add your own drawings to your collage.

STICKER PACKS: PicCollage EDU features hundreds of free stickers and backgrounds for your students to choose from.

FRAMES: If you want your students to create something quickly, have them select a frame to help generate an instant collage.

NO WATERMARKS OR ADS: PicCollage EDU does not contain any watermarks or ads, so everything is one hundred percent safe for classroom use.

SOCIAL MEDIA

WANT TO CONNECT?
Twitter: @PicCollage
Website: blog.piccollage.com/category/teachers-corner

VOCABULARY PRACTICE

GRADE LEVEL: Any

CONTENT AREA(S): Reading

COMFORT LEVEL: Medium

LESSON FORMAT: Student Created

QUICK TIP: Adding an "animation" will change the export file to a video file. This is handy if you're looking to upload to places like Flipgrid.

DESCRIPTION

Ditch the worksheet for this interACTIVE vocabulary lesson! Students can add multimedia to define vocabulary terms, and then save to the camera roll for easy access.

ISTE STANDARDS

- Students communicate complex ideas clearly and effectively by creating or using a variety of digital objects such as visualizations, models, or simulations. (6c)
- Students choose the appropriate platforms and tools for meeting the desired objectives of their creation or communication. (6a)

LESSON SUMMARY

1. Discuss your vocabulary terms as a whole group.
2. Display the vocabulary terms on the board. This works best using a PowerPoint or Google Slide and including an image with each vocabulary term.
3. Have the students open PicCollage EDU, and ask them to define each vocabulary term one at a time.
4. Encourage them to use a text box to define the word, along with other forms of multimedia (drawing, image, animation, etc.) to support their thinking.
5. Save each collage to the camera roll for easy access.

TRY APP SMASHING!

If your students have added animations, they can #AppSmash their collages into Flipgrid. Have each student post his or her first collage onto your grid. For the remainder of the vocabulary terms, ask them to respond directly to themselves. This will keep an organized thread so all terms are defined together.

NUMBER TALKS ON PICCOLLAGE EDU $1+1=2$

GRADE LEVEL: Any

CONTENT AREA(S): Math

COMFORT LEVEL: Beginner

LESSON FORMAT: Student Created

QUICK TIP: When starting this activity, ask your students to pick from one of the predesigned templates. Give them a collage separated into fourths and ask them to display four different strategies.

DESCRIPTION

Number Talks is a great way to strengthen your students' mental math. Integrate PicCollage to encourage your students to explain their thinking when sharing strategies.

ISTE STANDARDS

- Students use technology to seek feedback to inform and improve their practice and to demonstrate their learning in a variety of ways. (1c)
- Students communicate complex ideas clearly and effectively by creating or using a variety of digital objects such as visualizations, models, or simulations. (6c)

LESSON SUMMARY

1. Select a number you would like your students to work with.

2. After picking the number, explain to your students that they are to show you different ways to make the number. The challenge is to show as many possible ways within a selected amount of time.

3. Ask the students to open PicCollage EDU, and explain that they are permitted to use drawings, text boxes, and images to show their thinking.

4. Give the students time to complete the task.

5. When time is up, ask the students to save their collages on the device's camera roll.

6. Share the students' thinking with the rest of the class.

TRY APP SMASHING! Have your students upload their collage to Seesaw. This way you can get a view of how the entire class is doing as well as share their work with parents.

SILHOUETTE SUMMARIES

GRADE LEVEL: 3rd-5th

CONTENT AREA(S): Reading

COMFORT LEVEL: Medium

LESSON FORMAT: Student Created

QUICK TIP: Try downloading silhouette images to student iPads. Use the "airdrop" feature for fast sharing.

DESCRIPTION

Characterization just became more interACTIVE through the use of PicCollage EDU. Students describe a character or person, using the engaging multimedia features available through this student-friendly application.

ISTE STANDARDS

- Students curate information from digital resources, using a variety of tools and methods to create collections of artifacts to demonstrate meaningful connections or conclusions. (3c)

- Students create original works or responsibly repurpose or remix digital resources into new creations. (6b)

- Students communicate complex ideas clearly and effectively by creating or using a variety of digital objects, such as visualizations, models, or simulations. (6c)

LESSON SUMMARY

In PicCollage EDU, begin by going to "backgrounds." Select the silhouette image you wish to use.

- Students then describe the characters from the story, summarizing them through the use of images, words, stickers, and animations. Students can also search web images and choose from saved photos or GIFs.

- If, at any time, students wish to change or remove a photo, they can simply "drag and drop" it in the "trash can" icon at the top of the screen.

- When finished, click the "done" button in the top right corner and save.

Check out the animated image!

Start with character silhouette.

Summarize using text, images, and animations.

Check out the animated image!

GET STARTED NOW! SAVE THESE SILHOUETTE IMAGES TO YOUR CAMERA ROLL AND GET STARTED NOW WITH YOUR SUMMARIES!

BIBLIOGRAPHY

CHAPTER 1

Robinson, Sir Ken. 2006. TED2006. "Do schools kill creativity? Available at: ted.com/talks/ken_robinson_says_schools_kill_creativity."

CHAPTER 2

"Jean Piaget," FamousPsychologists.org, famouspsychologists.org/jean-piaget (accessed November 9, 2019).

MacKenzie, Trevor. 2019. *Dive into Inquiry: Amplify Learning and Empower Student Voice.* Victoria, BC, Canada: ElevateBooksEDU.

MacKenzie, Trevor, and Rebecca Bathurst-Hunt. 2019. *Inquiry Mindset: Nurturing the Dreams, Wonders, & Curiosities of Our Youngest Learners.* Victoria, BC, Canada: ElevateBooksEDU.

Spencer, John, and A. J. Juliani. 2017. *Empower: What Happens When Students Own Their Learning.* San Diego: IMpress.

CHAPTER 5

Cook, Julia, and Carrie Hartman. My Mouth Is a Volcano! Chattanooga, TN: National Center for Youth Issues, 2019.

Ferry, Beth, and Tom Lichtenheld. *Stick and Stone.* Boston: Houghton Mifflin Harcourt, 2018.

Javernick, Ellen, and Colleen M. Madden. *What If Everybody Did That?* Las Vegas: Two Lions, 2010.

Kranz, Linda, and Teresa Mlawer. *Only One You = Nadie Como tú.* Lanham, MD: Taylor Trade Publishing, 2015.

Ludwig, Trudy. *The Invisible Boy.* New York: Alfred A. Knopf, 2013.

Spires, Ashley. *The Most Magnificent Thing.* Toronto: Kids Can, 2017.

CHAPTER 6

Miller, Matt, and Alice Keeler. *Ditch That Homework: Practical Strategies to Help Make Homework Obsolete.* San Diego, CA: Dave Burgess Consulting, Incorporated, 2017.

CHAPTER 7

Stevens, Katrina. "Twitter Exec Reports that Educators Dominate the Twitter-sphere." *EdSurge,* April 30, 2014. edsurge.com/news/2014-04-30-twitter-exec-reports-that-educators-dominate-the-twitter-sphere.

PART TWO

Cook, Julia, and Kelsey De Weerd. *The Worst Day of My Life Ever!:* Nebraska: Boys Town Press, 2011.

Friedman, Laurie B., and Teresa Murfin. *Back-to-School Rules.* Minneapolis: Carolrhoda Books, 2011.

Henkes, Kevin. Lily's Purple Plastic Purse. New York: Greenwillow Books, 2006.

Javernick, Ellen, and Colleen M. Madden. *What If Everybody Did That?* Las Vegas: Two Lions, 2010.

Shannon, David. *No, David!* New York: Blue Sky, 1998.

ABOUT THE AUTHORS

Kristin and Joe share a love for Diet Coke, traveling, chocolate chip cookies, and well, each together. They have been married for eleven years, and they are blessed to be the parents of two sons—Bryson and Baxson. They live in Naples, Florida, and they teach at the same elementary school. They have a combined twenty-plus years of teaching experience, which they use as the foundation for the engaging lessons they collaborate to create.